Ordinary Differential Equations: Principles, Techniques, and Contemporary Perspectives

DR. KOMAL BANSAL

ASSISTANT PROFESSOR
MATHEMATICS

CENTER FOR DISTANCE AND ONLINE EDUCATION

CHANDIGARH UNIVERSITY

MOHALI, PUNJAB, INDIA
2025

"An equation means nothing to me unless it expresses a thought of God."

Srinivasa Ramanujan

Preface

Ordinary Differential Equations (ODEs) lie at the heart of mathematical modeling, bridging theory with applications across diverse scientific disciplines. From describing the growth of populations and the motion of celestial bodies to modeling economic systems and engineering dynamics, ODEs serve as indispensable tools for understanding and predicting real-world phenomena.

This book offers a comprehensive exploration of Ordinary Differential Equations (ODEs), emphasizing their foundational concepts, solution methods, and real-world applications. ODEs are vital in modeling phenomena across various fields, including physics, biology, engineering, and economics. The objective of this work is to provide both theoretical and practical insights into ODEs, guiding readers through the process of classification, solution techniques, and their applications.

The first chapter introduces the basic concepts of ODEs, starting with their definition and classification. It explores the process of forming differential equations by transforming a family of functions into an ODE, which is crucial for modeling real-world systems. The distinction between linear and nonlinear ODEs is made, with an emphasis on their different solution methods. The chapter also delves into the order and degree of ODEs, concepts that help categorize the equations. The order refers to the highest derivative in the equation, while the degree is the power of the highest derivative. Understanding these concepts is fundamental for solving ODEs and analyzing their complexity. Furthermore, the chapter discusses the importance of ODEs in various applications, such as in physics (e.g., motion and heat transfer) and engineering (e.g., electrical circuits and control systems).

The second chapter focuses on the methods of solving ODEs. It begins with the separation of variables technique, which is commonly used for first-order ODEs. This method involves separating the variables on each side of the equation and integrating both sides to obtain a solution. The chapter also covers homogeneous equations and total differential equations, introducing the concept of an integrating factor. An integrating factor is used to transform a non-exact equation into an exact one, making it solvable. Detailed explanations on how to find the integrating factor are provided, along with examples to illustrate its application.

Additionally, the second chapter explores first-order linear differential equations, which can be solved using the integrating factor method. The general approach for solving such equations is discussed, along with steps for handling non-homogeneous cases. Techniques for reducing equations to simpler forms are also included, which can aid in solving more complex ODEs by simplifying them into first-order linear equations.

The third chapter expands the discussion to second-order and higher-order differential equations. Solutions to second-order homogeneous equations with constant coefficients are covered in detail, with methods such as the characteristic equation and undetermined coefficients. The treatment of non-homogeneous second-order equations includes the use of symbolic functions to find particular integrals. Moreover, the chapter addresses the Cauchy-Euler equation and provides strategies for solving equations with variable coefficients.

The fourth chapter introduces the Wronskian, a determinant used to determine the linear independence of solutions in systems of linear differential equations. The Wronskian's properties and its role in constructing fundamental solution sets are explored, along with its application in solving linear systems of ODEs.

Finally, the book concludes with a discussion on the Sturm-Liouville boundary value problems, a class of eigenvalue problems that arise in various scientific fields. The chapter covers the theory of adjoint equations and Sturm theory, highlighting their importance in solving boundary value problems. The applications of these methods to real-world problems such as heat conduction and wave propagation are also discussed.

This book aims to equip readers with a solid understanding of ODEs, their solution techniques, and their wide range of applications, providing both the theoretical background and practical tools necessary for further study and research in this essential area of mathematics.

I hope that this book serves as a reliable guide and an enduring resource for those delving into the world of ordinary differential equations. May it inspire curiosity, foster understanding, and pave the way for further exploration in this rich and dynamic field.

Dr. Komal Bansal
Assistant Professor of Mathematics
Center for Distance and Online Education
Chandigarh University, Mohali, Punjab

Contents

Chapter 1

Foundations of Differential Equations

The art of proposing a question must be held of higher value than solving it.
— Georg Cantor

The origins of differential equations can be traced back to the invention of calculus by **Isaac Newton** and **Gottfried Wilhelm Leibniz** in the late 17th century. In Newton's work, particularly in his posthumously published *Methodus Fluxionum* (1736), he classified differential equations into three types:

- $\frac{dy}{dx} = f(x)$
- $\frac{dy}{dx} = f(x, y)$
- $x_1 \frac{\partial y}{\partial x_1} + x_2 \frac{\partial y}{\partial x_2} = y$

Leibniz also made significant contributions around the same time, introducing notation that is still in use today, including the integral sign and d for differentials. By 1693, both Newton and Leibniz had published their findings, marking the formal inception of differential equations as a distinct field in mathematics.

The 18th century saw substantial advancements in the theory and application of differential equations. Leonhard Euler made significant contributions to both ordinary and partial differential equations, developing methods for solving them and applying them to physical problems. Daniel Bernoulli used differential equations to model fluid dynamics and population growth. Joseph-Louis Lagrange contributed to the calculus of variations and furthered the understanding of second-order differential equations. During this period, much of the work revolved around geometric applications and mechanics, particularly in solving isoperimetric problems those involving optimization under constraints.

The 19th century marked a turning point with the introduction of more rigorous methods for solving differential equations. Augustin-Louis Cauchy emphasized the importance of proving the existence of solutions to differential equations. His work laid foundational principles for analysis and introduced methods that bridged calculus with complex variables. The introduction of Fourier series provided powerful tools for solving partial differential equations, particularly in heat conduction and wave propagation problems. This era also saw applications extend beyond classical mechanics into fields such as electricity and magnetism, influenced significantly by **James Clerk Maxwell**, whose equations unified electricity and magnetism through a set of partial differential equations.

In the 20th century, the study of differential equations continued to evolve with new theoretical frameworks and applications. The arrival of **set theory** influenced mathematical analysis, leading to a deeper understanding of function spaces and topological aspects related to solutions of ODEs. Applications expanded into areas such as quantum mechanics, dynamical systems, and relativity theory, showcasing the versatility of differential equations in modeling complex systems.

The history of differential equations illustrates a rich interplay between pure mathematics and applied sciences. From their early inception with Newton and Leibniz to their modern applications across various disciplines, differential equations have become fundamental tools for understanding dynamic systems. The ongoing research continues to unveil new connections with other mathematical fields, ensuring that this area remains vibrant and relevant.

1.1 Definition

Any equation between dependent variables, independent variables, or derivatives of the dependent variable with respect to the independent variable is called differential equation [1]. A differential equation is a mathematical equation that relates a function with its derivatives. It expresses how a quantity changes in relation to another variable, often representing physical phenomena such as motion, heat, and waves [2]. These equations play a fundamental role in modeling various physical, biological, and engineering systems. Consider

$$y = y(x), \quad y = y(x,t)$$

Here x and t are independent variables and y is dependent variable.
Examples:

$$\frac{d^2y}{dx^2} + y = e^x$$

$$\frac{\partial y}{\partial x} + \frac{\partial^2 y}{\partial t^2} = 0$$

1.2 Classification

- **Ordinary Differential Equations (ODEs):** Any differential equation in which **unique** independent variable contain total derivative of dependent variable with respect to independent variable is called ordinary differential equations. Equations involving functions of a single variable and their derivatives [3].

- **Partial Differential Equations (PDEs):** Equations involving partial derivatives of functions with multiple variables [4].

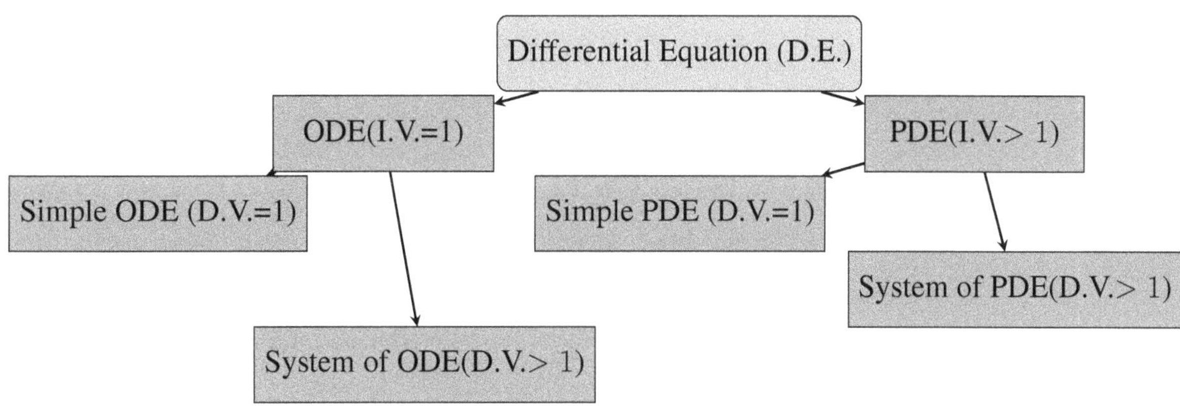

- **Simple ODE** Consider $y = y(x)$

$$\frac{d^2y}{dx^2} + y = e^x$$

- **System of ODE** Consider $y_1 = y_1(x), \quad y_2 = y_2(x)$

$$\frac{d^2y_1}{dx^2} + \frac{dy_2}{dx} = e^x$$

$$\frac{dy_1}{dx} + y\frac{dy_2}{dx} = e^x$$

- **Simple PDE** Consider $y = y(x,t)$

$$\frac{\partial y}{\partial x} + \frac{\partial^2 y}{\partial t^2} = 0$$

- **System of PDE** Consider $y_1 = y_1(x,t), \quad y_2 = y_2(x,t)$

$$\frac{\partial y_1}{\partial x} + \frac{\partial^2 y_2}{\partial t^2} = 0$$

$$\frac{\partial y_1}{\partial x} + \frac{\partial^2 y_2}{\partial t^2} = 0$$

1.3 Formation of ODE

The formation of ordinary differential equations involves identifying a family of functions, differentiating them, and eliminating arbitrary constants through substitution and further differentiation. This process is crucial in mathematical modeling across various fields, including physics and engineering, allowing us to describe dynamic systems effectively.

1.3.1 Steps to Form an ODE

1.3.1.1 Identify the Family of Functions

Start with an equation that includes arbitrary constants. For example, consider the family of straight lines given by the equation:

$$y = mx + c$$

where m and c are arbitrary constants.

1.3.1.2 Differentiate the Equation

Differentiate the equation with respect to the independent variable (in this case, x). This will help in eliminating the arbitrary constants. For the line equation:

$$\frac{dy}{dx} = m$$

1.3.1.3 Eliminate Arbitrary Constants

Use the original equation and its derivatives to eliminate the constants. From our example, we have:

- The original equation: $y = mx + c$
- The first derivative: $\frac{dy}{dx} = m$
- Rearranging gives $m = \frac{dy}{dx}$. Substitute this back into the original equation:$y = x\frac{dy}{dx} + c$

1.3.1.4 Differentiate Again if Necessary

If there are multiple arbitrary constants, differentiate again as needed, and eliminate all constants through substitution.

1.3.1.5 Resulting ODE

After eliminating all arbitrary constants, you will arrive at the ordinary differential equation.

Take a family of curves defined by n arbitrary constants. To derive an n-th order differential equation for which this family represents the solution, proceed as follows.

1.3.2 Working rule to form the differential equation:

- **Step I:** Begin by writing the equation that represents the given family of curves.
- **Step II:** Differentiate this equation n times to generate n additional equations, each involving the arbitrary constants and their derivatives.
- **Step III:** Eliminate the n arbitrary constants from the $n+1$ equations derived in Steps I and II. This process results in the required differential equation of order n.

Example 1: Differential Equation of $y = e^{mx}$

$$y = e^{mx},$$
$$\frac{dy}{dx} = me^{mx},$$
$$\frac{dy}{dx} = my, \quad m = \frac{1}{y} \cdot \frac{dy}{dx},$$
$$mx = \ln y, \quad m = \frac{\ln y}{x}.$$

Eliminating m, we get

$$\frac{1}{y} \cdot \frac{dy}{dx} = \frac{1}{x} \cdot \ln y.$$

Example 2: Differential Equations for Straight Lines

(a) Equation of any straight line passing through the origin is $y = mx$.

$$y = mx,$$
$$\frac{dy}{dx} = m.$$

Eliminating m, we get $y = x \cdot \frac{dy}{dx}$.

(b) Equation of any straight line in the xy-plane is $y = mx + c$.

$$y = mx + c,$$

$$\frac{dy}{dx} = m,$$
$$\frac{d^2y}{dx^2} = 0.$$

is the required differential equation.

Example 3

Given that $y = a\cos(mx - b)$.

Let's find the differential equation:

$$y = a\cos(mx - b)$$
$$\frac{dy}{dx} = -am\sin(mx - b)$$
$$\frac{d^2y}{dx^2} = -am^2\cos(mx - b)$$
$$\text{or} \quad \frac{d^2y}{dx^2} + m^2y = 0,$$

Thus, the required differential equation is $\frac{d^2y}{dx^2} + m^2y = 0$.

Example 4: Differential equation of all circles of radius a

The equation of all circles of radius a is given by

$$(x - h)^2 + (y - k)^2 = a^2$$

where h and k are arbitrary constants.

Differentiating with respect to x, we get

$$2(x - h) + 2(y - k)y' = 0$$

Again differentiating, we obtain

$$2 + 2(y')^2 + 2(y - k)y'' = 0 \quad \text{or} \quad y - k = -\frac{1 + (y')^2}{y''}$$

Substituting this value of $y - k$, we get

$$x - h = -(y - k)y' = \frac{1 + (y')^2}{y''}y'$$

$$\left(1 + (y')^2\right)^3 = a^2(y'')^2.$$

1.4 Order and Degree of Differential Equations

1.4.1 Order

The **order** of a differential equation is defined as the highest derivative of the dependent variable with respect to the independent variable present in the equation. It indicates the number of times the function is differentiated.

Example

Consider the following differential equations:

$$\frac{dy}{dx} = 3x + 2$$

- **Order**: 1 (the highest derivative is the first derivative $\frac{dy}{dx}$)

$$\frac{d^2y}{dx^2} + 2\frac{dy}{dx} + y = 0$$

- **Order**: 2 (the highest derivative is the second derivative $\frac{d^2y}{dx^2}$)

$$\frac{d^3y}{dx^3} + x\frac{dy}{dx} - y = e^x$$

- **Order**: 3 (the highest derivative is the third derivative $\frac{d^3y}{dx^3}$)

1.4.2 Degree

The **degree** of a differential equation is defined as the power of the highest order derivative in the equation when it is expressed as a polynomial in derivatives. The degree is only defined if the equation is a polynomial in derivatives.

Example

Using the same equations:

$$\frac{dy}{dx} = 3x + 2$$

- **Order**: 1, **Degree**: 1 (the first derivative $\frac{dy}{dx}$ is raised to the power of 1)

$$\frac{d^2y}{dx^2} + 2\frac{dy}{dx} + y = 0$$

- **Order**: 2, **Degree**: 1 (the highest order derivative $\frac{d^2y}{dx^2}$ is raised to the power of 1)

$$\left(\frac{d^2y}{dx^2}\right)^2 + x\left(\frac{dy}{dx}\right)^3 - y = e^x$$

- **Order**: 2, **Degree**: 2 (the highest order derivative $\frac{d^2y}{dx^2}$ is raised to the power of 2)

The **order** indicates how many times a function has been differentiated. The **degree** indicates the power to which the highest order derivative is raised, provided that the equation can be expressed as a polynomial in its derivatives. Understanding these concepts is crucial for solving and analyzing differential equations effectively.

1.5 Linear and Non-Linear Differential Equations

Understanding whether an ODE is linear or nonlinear is crucial for selecting appropriate methods for solving it, as linear equations typically have well-established solution techniques compared to their nonlinear counterparts.

A **linear ordinary differential equation** is defined as an equation that can be expressed in the form:

$$a_n(x)\frac{d^ny}{dx^n} + a_{n-1}(x)\frac{d^{n-1}y}{dx^{n-1}} + \ldots + a_1(x)\frac{dy}{dx} + a_0(x)y = b(x)$$

where $a_n(x), a_{n-1}(x), \ldots, a_0(x)$ and $b(x)$ are functions of the independent variable x, and y is the dependent variable. The key characteristic of linear ODEs is that the dependent variable y and its derivatives appear to the first power and are not multiplied together.

First-order linear ODE:

$$\frac{dy}{dx} + P(x)y = Q(x)$$

For instance:

$$\frac{dy}{dx} + 2y = \sin x$$

Second-order linear ODE:

$$\frac{d^2y}{dx^2} + 3\frac{dy}{dx} + 2y = 0$$

A **nonlinear ordinary differential equation** is any ODE that does not satisfy the criteria for linearity. This means that the dependent variable y or its derivatives appear with powers greater than one, or they are multiplied together, or they involve nonlinear functions (like sine, exponential, etc.).

First-order nonlinear ODE:

$$\frac{dy}{dx} = y^2 + x$$

Second-order nonlinear ODE:

$$\frac{d^2y}{dx^2} + y\frac{dy}{dx} = 0$$

- **Linear ODEs**: The dependent variable and its derivatives appear only to the first power, and there are no products of these terms.
- **Nonlinear ODEs**: The equation includes terms where the dependent variable or its derivatives are raised to powers greater than one or are multiplied together.

Find the order and degree of the following differential equations. Also classify them as linear and non-linear.

1. $y = x\frac{dy}{dx} - k\left(\frac{dy}{dx}\right)$

2. $y = x\frac{dy}{dx} - a\sqrt{1 - \left(\frac{dy}{dx}\right)^2}$

3. $\frac{dy}{dx} = y - \sin x$

4. $\left(\frac{d^2y}{dx^2}\right)^3 = x\left(\frac{dy}{dx}\right)^5 - y^2$

5. $\left\{y + x\left(\frac{dy}{dx}\right)^2\right\}^{4/3} = x\frac{d^2y}{dx^2}$

6. $\left(\frac{d^2y}{dx^2}\right)^{1/3} = \sqrt{y + \frac{dy}{dx}}$

1.6 Solution of Differential Equations

The solution of an ordinary differential equation refers to a function $y = \phi(x)$ that satisfies the equation for all values of the independent variable x in a given interval. Any relation between the dependent and independent variables, when substituted in the differential equation, reduces it to an identity is called a solution or integral of the differential equation. It should be noted that a solution of a differential equation does not involve the derivatives of the dependent variable with respect to the independent variable or variables. For example, $y = ce^{2x}$ is a solution of $\frac{dy}{dx} = 2y$. The solutions of ordinary differential equations (ODEs) can be classified into three main types: general solutions, particular solutions, and singular solutions. Below is a detailed definition of each type along with their characteristics.

1.6.1 General Solution

The **general solution** of a differential equation is a solution that contains all possible solutions of the equation. It typically includes arbitrary constants, which represent a family of solutions. The number of arbitrary constants in the general solution corresponds to the order of the differential equation. For example, the general solution of the first-order linear ODE:

$$\frac{dy}{dx} + P(x)y = Q(x)$$

can be expressed as:

$$y = Ce^{-\int P(x)dx}$$

where C is an arbitrary constant.

1.6.2 Particular Solution

A **particular solution** is derived from the general solution by assigning specific values to the arbitrary constants. This results in a specific function that satisfies both the differential equation and any initial or boundary conditions provided. For example, if the general solution is:

$$y = Cx^2 + 3$$

and if $y(1) = 5$, we can find C:

$$5 = C(1)^2 + 3 \implies C = 2$$

Thus, the particular solution is:

$$y = 2x^2 + 3$$

1.6.3 Singular Solution

A **singular solution** is a solution that cannot be obtained from the general solution by any choice of arbitrary constants. It often arises in cases where the differential equation has certain conditions or constraints that lead to unique behaviors not captured by the general solution. Singular solutions often occur in nonlinear equations. For example, consider the ODE:

$$y' = y^2$$

The general solution is:

$$y = -\frac{1}{x + C}$$

However, $y = 0$ is a singular solution because it satisfies the original equation but cannot be derived from the general form.

- For $y'' - 3y' + 2y = 0$, the general solution is $y = c_1 e^x + c_2 e^{2x}$, where c_1

and c_2 are independent arbitrary constants.

- Particular solutions are given by $y = e^x + e^{2x}$ and $y = e^x - 2e^{2x}$ etc.

- For $(dy/dx)^2 - 4y = 0$, the general solution is $y = (x - c)^2$. The singular solution is $y = 0$, which cannot be obtained by any choice of c in the general solution.

Understanding these types of solutions is crucial for effectively solving and interpreting ordinary differential equations in various applications.

1.7 Role in Modern Science and Engineering

Differential equations serve as a cornerstone in modeling phenomena in physics, chemistry, biology, and engineering. They describe dynamic systems, predict behaviors, and optimize processes [5–10].

Physical Sciences

- Newton's laws of motion, Maxwell's equations, and the Schr"odinger equation [11, 12].

- Wave, heat, and Laplace equations in various fields of physics [13, 14].

Biological Sciences

- Modeling population dynamics and epidemic spread [15–17].

- Chemical reaction rates and enzyme kinetics [16, 18–21].

Engineering Applications

- Control systems, signal processing, and circuit analysis [12, 22–24].

- Structural analysis and fluid dynamics in civil and mechanical engineering [2, 25].

The versatility of differential equations makes them integral to interdisciplinary studies:

- **Economics:** Modeling growth rates, supply-demand dynamics, and market equilibrium [26–28].
- **Environmental Science:** Describing pollutant dispersion and climate models [29–31].
- **Data Science:** Applications in machine learning and neural networks [25, 32].

1.8 Summary

In this introductory chapter, we have laid the groundwork for understanding differential equations by defining key concepts and classifications, including ordinary and partial differential equations, as well as the formation of ordinary differential equations (ODEs). We explored the essential steps in forming ODEs, the significance of order and degree, and distinguished between linear and non-linear equations. Furthermore, we discussed the types of solutions—general, particular, and singular—that arise from these equations, emphasizing their importance in both theoretical mathematics and practical applications across various fields such as physics, engineering, and economics. As we progress, we will delve deeper into methods for solving these equations, explore their applications in real-world scenarios, and examine advanced topics that highlight the ongoing relevance of differential equations in modern science and engineering.

Chapter 2

Methods of Solving Differential Equations

Life is a differential equation. It's just a matter of finding the solution.

This chapter focuses on various analytical methods used to solve ordinary differential equations (ODEs). These methods are essential for obtaining exact solutions to differential equations and include techniques such as separation of variables, homogeneous equations, and first-order linear equations [33, 34]. We will explore each method in detail, providing definitions, examples, and applications.

2.1 Separation of Variables

A differential equation is said to be **reducible to separation of variables** if it can be manipulated into the form:

$$\frac{dy}{dx} = f(x)g(y)$$

where $f(x)$ is a function of the independent variable x, and $g(y)$ is a function of the dependent variable y. Once in this form, the variables can be separated, allowing for straightforward integration. The **separation of variables** method is a powerful technique used to solve first-order ordinary differential equations that can be expressed in the form:

$$\frac{dy}{dx} = g(y)h(x)$$

Steps to Solve Using Separation of Variables

- Rearrange the equation to isolate y and x:

$$\frac{1}{g(y)}dy = h(x)dx$$

- Integrate both sides:

$$\int \frac{1}{g(y)}dy = \int h(x)dx$$

- Solve for y in terms of x.

Example

Consider the equation:

$$\frac{dy}{dx} = y^2 \sin(x)$$

1. Rearranging gives:

$$\frac{1}{y^2}dy = \sin(x)dx$$

2. Integrating both sides:

$$-\frac{1}{y} = -\cos(x) + C$$

3. Solving for y:

$$y = \frac{1}{\cos(x) - C}$$

Solve

- $\dfrac{dy}{dx} = e^{x-y} + x^2 e^{-y}$
- $\dfrac{dy}{dx} = y(-4x - xy^2)$

- $\dfrac{dy}{(y-1)(y-3)} = dx$

2.2 Reducible to Separation of Variables

Consider

$$\frac{dy}{dx} = f(ax + by + c)$$

Let $ax + by + c = t$

$$\begin{aligned} a + b\frac{dy}{dx} &= \frac{dt}{dx} \\ \frac{dy}{dx} &= \frac{1}{b}\left(\frac{dt}{dx} - a\right) \\ \frac{1}{b}\left(\frac{dt}{dx} - a\right) &= f(t) \\ \frac{dt}{dx} &= a + bf(t) \\ \frac{dt}{a + bf(t)} &= dx \end{aligned}$$

To reduce a differential equation to a separable form, follow these general steps:

- Identify the Equation: Start with a differential equation that may not initially appear to be separable.
- Perform Substitutions: Use appropriate substitutions to transform the equation into a separable form. Common substitutions include: - $v = ax + by + c$ for equations of the form $\frac{dy}{dx} = f(ax + by + c)$.
- Rearrange and Separate: Rearrange the equation to isolate terms involving y on one side and terms involving x on the other side.
- Integrate: Integrate both sides separately.

Example

1. Consider the following differential equation:

$$\frac{dy}{dx} = \sin(x + y)$$

Let $v = x + y$. Then, we have:

$$y = v - x \quad \text{and} \quad \frac{dy}{dx} = \frac{dv}{dx} - 1$$

Substituting into the original equation gives:

$$\frac{dv}{dx} - 1 = \sin(v)$$

Rearranging leads to:

$$\frac{dv}{dx} = \sin(v) + 1$$

Now, separate variables:

$$\frac{1}{\sin(v) + 1} dv = dx$$

Integrate both sides:

$$\int \frac{1}{\sin(v) + 1} dv = \int dx$$

The left-hand side requires specific techniques or tables for integration, while the right-hand side integrates simply to $x + C$. Differential equations that can be reduced to separation of variables provide an effective pathway to finding solutions through integration. By identifying suitable substitutions and manipulating the equation into a separable format, one can simplify complex ODEs into manageable forms.

2. $\frac{dy}{dx} = (4x + y + 1)^2$
Let

$$4x + y + 1 = v$$

Differentiating with respect to x, we get

$$4 + \frac{dy}{dx} = \frac{dv}{dx}$$

or

$$\frac{dy}{dx} = \frac{dv}{dx} - 4.$$

$\frac{dv}{dx} - 4 = v^2$ or $\frac{dv}{dx} = 4 + v^2$.

Now, separating variables x and v, $dx = \frac{dv}{4+v^2}$.

Integrating, $x + c_1 = \frac{1}{2}\tan^{-1}\left(\frac{v}{2}\right)$, where c_1 is an arbitrary constant.

3. **Solve:** $\frac{dy}{dx} = \frac{a^2}{(x+y)^2}$

2.3 Homogeneous Equations

A first-order differential equation is called **homogeneous** if it can be expressed in the form:

$$\frac{dy}{dx} = F\left(\frac{y}{x}\right)$$

This means that the right-hand side is a function of the ratio $\frac{y}{x}$. Such equations can often be solved by making the substitution $v = \frac{y}{x}$, leading to separable variables. A function $f(x, y)$ is called homogeneous function of degree n if $f(\lambda x, \lambda y) = \lambda^n f(x, y)$.

- $f(x, y) = 5x^3 + 2x^2y + 3y^3$
- $f(x, y) = e^{\frac{x+y}{2x-y}}$
- $f(x, y) = xcosec\left(\frac{y}{x}\right) - y$

Let $\lambda = \frac{1}{x}$

$$f\left(1, \frac{y}{x}\right) = \frac{1}{x^n} f(x, y)$$
$$f(x, y) = x^n f\left(1, \frac{y}{x}\right)$$
$$f(x, y) = x^n g\left(\frac{y}{x}\right)$$

Now, consider the D.E. $f_1(x,y)dx + f_2(x,y)dy = 0$ in which $f_1(x,y)$ and $f_2(x,y)$ are homogeneous functions of the same degree n.

$$\frac{dy}{dx} = \frac{-f_1(x,y)}{f_2(x,y)}$$

$$\frac{dy}{dx} = \phi\left(\frac{y}{x}\right)$$

Let $\frac{y}{x} = v \implies y = vx$

$$\frac{dy}{dx} = v + x\frac{dv}{dx} = \phi(v)$$

$$\frac{dv}{\phi(v) - v} = \frac{dx}{x} \implies F(v) = logx + c$$

Steps to Solve Homogeneous Equations

- Substitute $v = \frac{y}{x}$, which implies $y = vx$.
- Differentiate using the product rule:

$$\frac{dy}{dx} = v + x\frac{dv}{dx}$$

- Substitute back into the original equation and simplify.
- Separate variables and integrate.

Example:
Consider the equation:

$$\frac{dy}{dx} = \frac{y^2 + x^2}{xy}$$

Substitute $v = \frac{y}{x}$, then $y = vx$:

$$\frac{dy}{dx} = v + x\frac{dv}{dx}$$

The equation becomes:

$$v + x\frac{dv}{dx} = \frac{(vx)^2 + x^2}{vx.x}$$

Simplifying leads to:

$$vdv = \frac{dx}{x}$$

Separate variables and integrate.
Solve:

- $x\frac{dy}{dx} = y(logy - logx + 1)$
- $(y + \sqrt{x^2 + y^2})dx - xdy = 0$

2.4 General Approach to Reducing to Homogeneous Form

To reduce a non-homogeneous differential equation to homogeneous form, follow these steps:

- **Identify the Equation:** Start with a differential equation that may not initially appear to be homogeneous.
- **Perform Substitutions:** Use appropriate substitutions to eliminate constants and transform the equation into a homogeneous form. Common substitutions include: - $x = X + h$ - $y = Y + k$ Here, h and k are constants chosen to make the equation homogeneous.
- **Rearrange and Simplify:** After substitution, simplify the equation so that all terms are expressed in terms of X and Y.
- **Check Homogeneity:** Ensure that the resulting equation is homogeneous in terms of X and Y.

Example

Consider the differential equation:

$$\frac{dy}{dx} = \frac{x + 2y - 3}{2x + y - 3}$$

Step 1: Identify Constants

The constants in this equation (i.e., -3) suggest that we need to eliminate them to achieve homogeneity.

Step 2: Perform Substitutions

We will make substitutions as follows: Let: $x = X + h$, $y = Y + k$

We need to choose h and k such that the constants cancel out.

Step 3: Choose Constants

To eliminate the constant -3 from both the numerator and denominator, we set up the following equations:

1. From the numerator:

$$h + 2k - 3 = 0$$

2. From the denominator:

$$2h + k - 3 = 0$$

Solving these equations simultaneously will give us values for h and k.

From the first equation:

$$k = \frac{3 - h}{2}$$

Substituting this into the second equation:

$$2h + \left(\frac{3 - h}{2}\right) - 3 = 0$$

Multiplying through by 2 to eliminate the fraction gives:

$$4h + (3 - h) - 6 = 0$$

Simplifying:

$$3h - 3 = 0 \implies h = 1$$

Substituting $h = 1$ back into one of our equations to find k:

$$k = \frac{3 - 1}{2} = 1$$

Thus, we have $h = 1$ and $k = 1$.

Step 4: Substitute Back into the Equation

Now substituting back into our original variables: Substitute $x = X + 1$, $y = Y + 1$

The differential equation becomes:

$$\frac{dy}{dx} = \frac{(X + 1) + 2(Y + 1) - 3}{2(X + 1) + (Y + 1) - 3}$$

Simplifying gives:

Numerator:

$$X + 1 + 2Y + 2 - 3 = X + 2Y$$

Denominator:

$$2X + 2 + Y + 1 - 3 = 2X + Y$$

So now we have:

$$\frac{dY}{dX} = \frac{X + 2Y}{2X + Y}$$

This is now in homogeneous form.

Step 5: Solve the Homogeneous Equation

Now we can use the substitution $v = \frac{Y}{X}$:

Thus,

$$Y = vX \implies dY/dX = v + X(dv/dX)$$

Substituting this back into our homogeneous equation gives us:

$$v + X\frac{dv}{dX} = \frac{X + 2(vX)}{2X + vX}$$

From here, you can separate variables and integrate to find solutions. By following these steps, we have successfully transformed a non-homogeneous differential equation into a homogeneous form, allowing us to apply methods for solving such equations effectively. This process illustrates how careful manipulation and substitution can simplify complex problems in differential equations.

Solve

- $\frac{dy}{dx} = \frac{x + y + 1}{x + y - 1}$
- $(2x + y + 1)dx + (x + 2y - 1)dy = 0$
- $\frac{dy}{dx} = \frac{2x + y + 3}{x + 2y + 4}$

2.5 Total Differential Equations

In this section, we will discuss total differential equations, the concept of integrating factors, and the working rules for finding integrating factors. This knowledge is crucial for solving first-order ordinary differential equations (ODEs) that may not be immediately separable or exact.

A **total differential equation** is an expression that describes the change in a multivariable function with respect to its independent variables [35, 36]. For a function $z = f(x, y)$, the total differential is given by:

$$dz = \frac{\partial f}{\partial x}dx + \frac{\partial f}{\partial y}dy$$

This equation represents how the function z changes with small changes in x and y. The total differential captures both the direct and indirect effects of changes in the independent variables on the dependent variable.

Let F be a function of two real variable such that F has continuous first partial derivative in domain D then the total differential of F is denoted by dF and is given by the expression

$$dF = \frac{\partial F}{\partial x}dx + \frac{\partial F}{\partial y}dy \ \forall\, x, y \in D.$$

Let $F(x, y) = x^3 \sin y + y^2x^2$

$$\implies dF = (3x^2 \sin y + 2xy^2)dx + (x^3 \cos y + 2yx^2)dy$$

$$\implies dF = d(x^3 \sin y + y^2x^2) \ \forall\, x, y \in D$$

The expression $Mdx + Ndy$ is called exact differential form if $\exists$ a function F, called potential function then $dF = Mdx + Ndy \ \forall x, y \in D$.

Note:

- The expression $Mdx + Ndy$ is called exact differential form if $\exists$ a function F, called potential function define on domain D such that $\dfrac{\partial F}{\partial x} = M;\ \dfrac{\partial F}{\partial y} = N$.
- If $Mdx + Ndy$ is exact differential form then the equation is called exact differential equation.
- Let M, N, $\dfrac{\partial M}{\partial y}, \dfrac{\partial N}{\partial x}$ are continuous function in domain D, then the equation $Mdx + Ndy = 0$ is called exact differential equation iff $\dfrac{\partial M}{\partial y} = \dfrac{\partial N}{\partial x}$.
- It is necessary and sufficient condition for the differential equation to be exact.

Example: For what values of a and b, $(x^2 - ay)dx + (y^2 - bx) = 0$ is exact differential equation.

Example: Find the function $f(x, y)$ such that the differential equation $f(x, y)dx + (2ye^x + y^2e^{3x})dy = 0$ is exact differential equation.

Let $Mdx + Ndy = 0$ be the exact differential equation then the following are the solution of the differential equation:

- $$\int_{y \text{ constant}} Mdx + \int_{N \text{ free from x}} Ndy = C$$
- $$\int_{x \text{ constant}} Ndy + \int_{M \text{ free from y}} Mdx = C$$
- $$\int Mdx + \int \left(N - \frac{\partial}{\partial y} \int Mdx \right) dy = C$$
- $$\int Ndy + \int \left(M - \frac{\partial}{\partial x} \int Ndy \right) dx = C$$

Solve

- $e^y dx + (xe^y + y)dy = 0$
- $-y \sin 2x dx + \cos^2 x dy = 0$

2.5.1 Integrating Factor

An **integrating factor** is a function that is used to convert a non-exact differential equation into an exact one. If we have a first-order linear differential equation of the form:

$$M(x, y) + N(x, y)\frac{dy}{dx} = 0$$

where M and N are functions of x and y, the equation is said to be exact if there exists a function $F(x, y)$ such that:

$$\frac{\partial F}{\partial x} = M \quad \text{and} \quad \frac{\partial F}{\partial y} = N$$

If the equation is not exact, we can find an integrating factor $\mu(x, y)$ such that multiplying through by this factor makes the equation exact:

$$\mu(x,y)(M + N\frac{dy}{dx}) = 0$$

- Let $Mdx + Ndy = 0$ be a non-exact differential equation and $\phi(x,y)$ be a function such that $\phi(x,y)(Mdx + Ndy) = 0$ be the exact differential equation then $\phi(x,y)$ is called integrating factor.

- **Example:** $xdy - ydx = 0$ is not an exact differential equation.

$$\textbf{I.F.} \quad \frac{1}{x^2}, \frac{1}{y^2}, \frac{1}{x^2+y^2}, \frac{1}{xy}$$

- $\phi(x,y)$ be integrating factor then any constant multiple of IF is also an I.F.

- Every linear combination of the integrating factor is also an integrating factor.

2.5.2 Working Rule to Find Integrating Factor

To find an integrating factor, we can use several methods depending on the form of the differential equation:

For Linear First-Order ODEs: If the equation can be written in the standard form:

$$\frac{dy}{dx} + P(x)y = Q(x)$$

The integrating factor $\mu(x)$ is given by:

$$\mu(x) = e^{\int P(x)dx}$$

For Exact Equations: If you have an equation of the form:

$$M(x,y) + N(x,y)\frac{dy}{dx} = 0$$

Check if:

$$\frac{\partial M}{\partial y} = \frac{\partial N}{\partial x}$$

If not, look for an integrating factor that depends only on x or y.

For Non-Exact Equations:

If $\dfrac{M_y - N_x}{N} = h(x)$, then an integrating factor can often be found as:

$$\mu(x) = e^{\int g(y)dy}$$

If $\dfrac{-M_y + N_x}{M} = g(y)$, then an integrating factor can often be found as:

$$\mu(y) = e^{\int g(y)dx}$$

For Homogeneous Functions: If both $M(x, y)$ and $N(x, y)$ are homogeneous functions of the same degree, then an integrating factor can often be found as:

$$\mu(x, y) = (x^a)(y^b)$$

Let $Mdx + Ndy = 0$ be the non exact differential equation. Let $\phi(x, y) = \phi(v)$ be an integrating factor where v be the known function of x & y.
$\phi(v)(Mdx + Ndy) = 0$ is exact differential equation.

$$\frac{\phi'(v)}{\phi(v)} = \frac{N_x - M_y}{v_y M - v_x N} = f(v)$$

$\phi(v) = e^{\int f(v)dv}$ is an integrating factor.

- If $xM + yN \neq 0$ and D.E. is homogeneous then I.F. is $\dfrac{1}{xM + yN}$.
- If $xM - yN \neq 0$ and D.E. can be written as $yf_1(x, y)dx + xf_2(x, y)dy = 0$ then I.F. $\dfrac{1}{xM - yN}$.
- If $\dfrac{M_y - N_x}{N} = f(x)$ or constant then I.F. is $e^{\int f(x)}dx$.
- If $\dfrac{-M_y + N_x}{M} = f(y)$ or constant then I.F. is $e^{\int f(y)}dy$.
- If $x^a y^b(mydx + nxdy) + x^{a'} y^{b'}(m'ydx + n'xdy) = 0$. Let I.F. is $x^h y^k$

where h and k is given by

$$\frac{a+h+1}{m}=\frac{b+k+1}{n} \text{ or } \frac{a'+h+1}{m}=\frac{b'+k+1}{n}$$

Example

Consider the differential equation:

$$(2xy+3y^2)dx+(x^2+3xy)\frac{dy}{dx}=0$$

To find an integrating factor:
1. Check if it is exact: Let $M=2xy+3y^2, \quad N=x^2+3xy$
2. Calculate: $M_y=2x+6y, \quad N_x=2x+3y$ Since $M_y \neq N_x$, it's not exact.
3. Find an integrating factor based on dependence on one variable or homogeneity.
Solve:

- If I.F. of the D.E. $(x^7y^2+3y)dx+(3x^8y-x)dy=0$ is x^my^n then find m and n.

- Find I.F. for the D.E. $cosy.sin2xdx+(cos^2y-cos^2x)dy=0$.

By applying these rules systematically, you can identify and apply integrating factors to solve non-exact differential equations effectively. Total differential equations and integrating factors are vital tools in solving ordinary differential equations. Understanding how to identify when an integrating factor is needed and how to compute it allows for greater flexibility in tackling a wide range of problems in mathematics and applied fields.

2.6 First-Order Linear Differential Equations

A first-order linear differential equation can be written in the standard form:

$$\frac{dy}{dx}+P(x)y=Q(x)$$

Let $\dfrac{dy}{dx} = f(x,y) \implies \dfrac{dy}{dx} = P(x)y + Q(x)$ or $\dfrac{dy}{dx} + P(x)y = Q(x)$

$$dy + (P(x)y - Q(x))dx = 0$$

$\implies M_y = P \;\&\; N_x = 0$

$$\frac{M_y - N_x}{N} = P(x) \implies \text{I.F.} = e^{\int P(x)dx}.$$

Then $e^{\int P(x)dx}\dfrac{dy}{dx} + P(x)e^{\int P(x)dx}y = e^{\int P(x)dx}Q(x)$

$$\implies d(e^{\int P(x)dx}y) = e^{\int P(x)dx}Q(x)$$

$$\implies e^{\int P(x)dx}.y = \int e^{\int P(x)dx}Q(x)dx + C$$

$$\implies IF.y = \int IF.Q(x)dx + C$$

If $Q(x) = 0 \;\forall\; x$, then $\dfrac{dy}{dx} + P(x)y = 0$
$\implies e^{\int P(x)dx}.y = C$
$\implies y = Ce^{-\int P(x)dx} = Ce^{F(x)}$
Let $y(x_0) = y_0 \implies C = y_0e^{-F(x_0)}$

$$\implies y(x) = y_0e^{f(x)}e^{-F(x_0)}$$

is identically zero or never zero.

2.6.1 Steps to Solve First-Order Linear ODEs:

1. Identify $P(x)$ and $Q(x)$.
2. Calculate the integrating factor:

$$I(x) = e^{\int P(x)dx}$$

3. Multiply the entire equation by the integrating factor.
4. Rewrite the left side as a derivative:

$$I(x)\frac{dy}{dx} + I(x)P(x)y = I(x)Q(x)$$

5. Integrate both sides.

Example

Consider the equation:

$$\frac{dy}{dx} + 3y = 6$$

1. Identify $P(x) = 3$ and $Q(x) = 6$.
2. Calculate the integrating factor:

$$I(x) = e^{\int 3dx} = e^{3x}$$

3. Multiply through by the integrating factor:

$$e^{3x}\frac{dy}{dx} + 3e^{3x}y = 6e^{3x}$$

4. Rewrite as a derivative:

$$\frac{d}{dx}(e^{3x}y) = 6e^{3x}$$

5. Integrate both sides:

$$e^{3x}y = 2e^{3x} + C$$

6. Solve for y:

$$y = 2 + Ce^{-3x}$$

Solve

1. $(1 + y^2) + (x - e^{tan^{-1}y})\dfrac{dy}{dx} = 0$
2. $\dfrac{dy}{dx} + \dfrac{2x+1}{x}y = e^{-2x} : x > 0$
3. $\dfrac{dy}{dx} - ay = e^{ax} \;\&\; y(0) = 0$

Existence and Uniqueness Consider $\dfrac{dy}{dx} + P(x)y = Q(x)$,

- If $P(x)$ and $Q(x)$ are continuous and bounded then D.E. always has a solution.
- If $P(x)$ and $Q(x)$ are integrable then D.E. always has solution.
- Consider the D.E. $\dfrac{dy}{dx} + P(x)y = Q(x)$ & $y(x_0) = y_0$ define on an interval I and if $P(x)$ and $Q(x)$ are continuous and bounded on I then D.E. always has a unique solution on an interval I.
- The condition of continuity and bounded is sufficient condition not necessarily.

Example

- $\dfrac{dy}{dx} + y = f(x); y(0) = 0 \; \forall \; x$ where

$$f(x) = \begin{cases} 2; & 0 \le x \le 1 \\ 0; & x > 1 \end{cases}$$

- $\dfrac{dy}{dx} + 2y = f(x); y(0) = 0 \; \forall \; x$ where

$$f(x) = \begin{cases} 1; & 0 \le x \le 1 \\ 0; & x > 1 \end{cases}$$

2.6.2 Reducible to Linear Differential Equation

Consider

$$f'(y)\frac{dy}{dx} + f(y)P(x) = Q(x).$$

Let $f(y) = t \implies f'(y)\dfrac{dy}{dx} = \dfrac{dt}{dx}$

$$\implies \frac{dt}{dx} + P(x)t = Q(x)$$

which is linear differential equation in t.

Example

- $\frac{dy}{dx} + \tan y \tan x = \cos x \sec y$
- $\sec^2 y \frac{dy}{dx} + 2x \tan y = x^3$

subsectionBernoulli's Equation Consider

$$\frac{dy}{dx} + P(x)y = Q(x)y^n : n \neq 0, 1$$

$$y^{-n}\frac{dy}{dx} + P(x)y^{-n+1} = Q(x)$$

Let

$$y^{1-n} = t \implies (1-n)y^{(-n)}\frac{dy}{dx} = \frac{dt}{dx}$$

$$\implies y^{-n}\frac{dy}{dx} = \frac{1}{(1-n)}\frac{dt}{dx}$$

$$\implies \frac{1}{(1-n)}\frac{dt}{dx} + P(x)t = Q(x)$$

$$\implies \frac{dt}{dx} + (1-n)P(x)t = (1-n)Q(x)$$

which is linear differential equation in t.

Example

- $\frac{dy}{dx} = ay - by^2$ where $a, b > 0$ and $y(0) = y_0$
- $\frac{dy}{dx} = xy + y^2x^3$ and $y(0) = 1$

2.7 Conclusion

In this chapter, we explored several analytical methods for solving ordinary differential equations, including separation of variables, homogeneous equations, and first-order linear equations. Each method provides a systematic approach to finding exact solutions, which are crucial in various applications across science and engineering.

Chapter 3

Second-Order and Higher-Order Differential Equations

Life is like a differential equation; to find solutions, you must understand the variables.

Second-order and higher-order ordinary differential equations (ODEs) play a crucial role in mathematical modeling across various fields of science and engineering. This chapter focuses on the classification, solution methods, and applications of these equations. We will discuss both constant and variable coefficient equations, Cauchy-Euler equations, and the techniques for finding complementary functions and particular integrals [37–39].

3.1 Second-Order Differential Equations

A second-order differential equation can be expressed in the general form:

$$a(x)\frac{d^2y}{dx^2} + b(x)\frac{dy}{dx} + c(x)y = f(x)$$

where $a(x)$, $b(x)$, and $c(x)$ are continuous functions on an interval, and $f(x)$ is a given function.

3.1.1 Homogeneous Second-Order Differential Equations

A second-order ODE is called **homogeneous** if $f(x) = 0$:

$$a(x)\frac{d^2y}{dx^2} + b(x)\frac{dy}{dx} + c(x)y = 0$$

3.1.1.1 Constant Coefficients

For constant coefficients, the equation takes the form:

$$ay'' + by' + cy = 0$$

The characteristic equation associated with this ODE is:

$$ar^2 + br + c = 0$$

The roots of this characteristic equation determine the general solution:
- **Distinct Real Roots**: If r_1 and r_2 are distinct real roots:

$$y = C_1e^{r_1x} + C_2e^{r_2x}$$

- **Repeated Roots**: If r is a repeated root:

$$y = (C_1 + C_2x)e^{rx}$$

- **Complex Roots**: If $r = \alpha \pm \beta i$:

$$y = e^{\alpha x}(C_1\cos(\beta x) + C_2\sin(\beta x))$$

Example: Solve $y'' - 5y' + 6y = 0$

$$r^2 - 5r + 6 = 0 \implies (r-2)(r-3) = 0$$

Roots: $r_1 = 2$, $r_2 = 3$

$$y = C_1e^{2x} + C_2e^{3x}$$

Solve

- $y'' + 3y' - 10y = 0$
- $y'' + 2y' + y = 0$
- $y'' - 6y' + 25y = 0$

Note

- **Unique solution** exists when $y(x_0) = y_0$ & $y'(x_0) = y_1$.
- **Infinite solution** exists if we get one constant and solution depend on arbitrary constant.
- **No solution** exists when conditions are not satisfied.
- $y'' + ay' + by = 0$ always has a bounded solution which is $y(x) = 0$.
- If root of the D.E. are real and distinct (equal) then non-trivial solution is never bounded.
- Every solution of differential equation is bounded and periodic if roots are purely imaginary $(a = 0, b > 0)$.

3.1.2 Non-Homogeneous Second-Order Differential Equations

A second-order ODE is called **non-homogeneous** if $f(x) \neq 0$:

$$ay'' + by' + cy = f(x)$$

The general solution is given by:

$$y = y_h + y_p$$

where y_h is the complementary function (solution of the homogeneous equation), and y_p is a particular integral (solution of the non-homogeneous equation).

3.1.2.1 The Symbolic Function $\frac{1}{f(D)}$

The expression

$$\frac{1}{f(D)}X$$

is defined to be that function of x which, when operated upon by $f(D)$, gives X.

For example,

$$\frac{1}{D^2+3D}\cdot(2+6x)=x^2.$$

The operator $\frac{1}{f(D)}$, according to this definition, is the inverse of the operator $f(D)$. Thus, $\frac{1}{D}X=\int X\,dx$.

3.1.2.2 Particular Integral (P.I.) of $f(D)y = X$

The particular integral of

$$f(D)y=X$$

is given by

$$\text{P.I.}=\frac{1}{f(D)}X.$$

General Approach to Obtaining the Particular Integral

Theorem 3.1.1. *If X is a function of x, then*

$$\frac{1}{f(D)}X=e^x\int e^{-x}X\,dx.$$

3.1.2.3 Short Methods for Finding the P.I.

The general approach to determining the particular integral (P.I.) often involves lengthy calculations in many cases. However, the P.I. can be derived more efficiently using shorter methods when X takes one of the following specific forms:

3.1.2.4 $X = e^{ax}$, where a is any constant

If $f(a)\neq 0$,

$$P.I.=\frac{e^{ax}}{f(D)}f(a)$$

If $f(a) = 0$,

$$P.I. = \frac{x^n e^{ax}}{D^n f(a)}$$

where $D^n f(a)$ denotes the nth derivative of $f(D)$ evaluated at $D = a$.

3.1.2.5 $X = \sin(ax)$ or $X = \cos(ax)$

When $f(D^2)$ can be expressed as $D^2 + a^2$ and $f(-a^2) \neq 0$

$$\frac{1}{f(D^2)} \sin ax = \frac{1}{f(-a^2)} \sin ax$$
$$\frac{1}{f(D^2)} \cos ax = \frac{1}{f(-a^2)} \cos ax$$

Thus, the rule is to replace D^2 by $-a^2$.

When $f(D^2) = D^2 + a^2$ and $f(-a^2) = -a^2 + a^2 = 0$. However,

$$P.I. = \frac{1}{D^2 + a^2} \sin(ax)$$

is equal to the imaginary part of

$$P.I. = \frac{1}{D^2 + a^2} \left(e^{iax}\right),$$

3.1.2.6 $X = x^n$ or a polynomial

$X = a_0 x^n + a_1 x^{n-1} + \ldots + a_{n-1} x + a_n$ where n is any positive integer.

Working Rule for Evaluating $\frac{1}{f(D)} x^m$

Step I. Extract the term with the lowest degree from $f(D)$, ensuring that the remaining factor in the denominator takes the form $[1 \pm \phi(D)]^n$, n where n is a positive integer.

Step II. Take $[1 \pm \phi(D)]^n$ in the numerator so that it takes the form $[1 \pm \phi(D)]^{-n}$.

Step III. Expand $[1 \pm \phi(D)]^{-n}$ by the binomial theorem, namely:

$$(1 + x)^n = 1 + nx + \frac{n(n-1)}{2!} x^2 + \frac{n(n-1)(n-2)}{3!} x^3 + \cdots$$

In particular, the following binomial expansions should be remembered:

$$(1-x)^{-1} = 1 + x + x^2 + x^3 + \cdots,$$

$$(1+x)^{-1} = 1 - x + x^2 - x^3 + \cdots,$$

$$(1-x)^{-2} = 1 + 2x + 3x^2 + 4x^3 + \cdots,$$

$$(1+x)^{-2} = 1 - 2x + 3x^2 - 4x^3 + \cdots.$$

In any case, the expansion is to be carried up to D^m, since:

$$D^m x^m = m!,$$

$$D^{m+1} x^m = 0,$$

and all higher-order differential coefficients of x^m become zero. If instead of x^m, we have a polynomial $x^m + a_1 x^{m-1} + \cdots + a_{m-1}x + a_m$ of degree m, the evaluation of $\frac{1}{f(D)}(x^m + a_1 x^{m-1} + \cdots + a_{m-1}x + a_m)$ proceeds in the same way as for $\frac{1}{f(D)}x^m$. Similarly, if X is a constant, this method remains applicable.

3.1.2.7 $X = x^n V$, where V is a function of x and n is a positive integer

$$\frac{1}{f(D)} e^{ax} V = e^{ax} \cdot \frac{1}{f(D+a)} V,$$

where V is a function of x. Accordingly, e^{ax}, which is on the right of $\frac{1}{f(D)}$, may be taken to the left provided D is replaced by $D + a$.

3.2 Variable Coefficient Second-Order Differential Equations

For variable coefficients, we consider equations of the form:

$$y'' + p(x)y' + q(x)y = g(x)$$

3.2.1 Cauchy-Euler Equation

A specific type of second-order linear differential equation with variable coefficients is called a **Cauchy-Euler equation**, which has the form:

$$x^2y'' + axy' + by = f(x)$$

Consider $x^2y'' + axy' + by = 0; \quad x > 0$
Let $x = e^z \implies z = logx$

$$\frac{dy}{dx} = \frac{dy}{dx}\frac{dz}{dz} = \frac{dy}{dz}\frac{dz}{dx} = \frac{1}{x}\frac{dy}{dz}$$

$$\implies x\frac{dy}{dx} = \frac{dy}{dz}$$

Now,

$$\frac{d^2y}{dx^2} = \frac{d}{dx}\left(\frac{dy}{dx}\right) = \frac{d}{dx}\left(\frac{1}{x}\frac{dy}{dz}\right) = \frac{1}{x}\frac{d}{dx}\left(\frac{dy}{dz}\right) - \frac{1}{x^2}\frac{dy}{dz}$$

$$\frac{d^2y}{dx^2} = \frac{1}{x}\frac{d}{dz}\left(\frac{dy}{dz}\frac{dz}{dx}\right) - \frac{1}{x^2}\frac{dy}{dz} = \frac{1}{x^2}\frac{d^2y}{dz^2} - \frac{1}{x^2}\frac{dy}{dz}$$

$$\implies x^2\frac{d^2y}{dx^2} = \frac{d^2y}{dz^2} - \frac{dy}{dz} \implies \frac{d^2y}{dz^2} + (a-1)\frac{dy}{dz} + by = 0$$

which is linear differential equation with constant coefficient.

- **If roots are real and distinct:** $y(z) = c_1e^{\lambda_1 z} + c_2e^{\lambda_2 z} \implies y(x) = c_1x^{\lambda_1} + c_2x^{\lambda_2}$

- **If roots are real and equal:** $y(z) = (c_1 + c_2z)e^{\lambda_1 z} \implies y(x) = (c_1 + c_2logx)x^{\lambda_1}$

- **If roots are complex:** $y(z) = e^{\alpha z}(c_1\cos\beta z + c_2\sin\beta z) \implies y(x) = x^{\alpha}(c_1\cos\beta logx + c_2\sin\beta logx)$

- General solution is never periodic.

- Every solution of differential equation is bounded if roots are purely imaginary $(a-1=0, b>0)$.

A linear differential equation of the form

$$a_0x^n\frac{d^ny}{dx^n}+a_1x^{n-1}\frac{d^{n-1}y}{dx^{n-1}}+\cdots+a_{n-1}x\frac{dy}{dx}+a_ny=X$$

i.e.,

$$(a_0x^nD^n+a_1x^{n-1}D^{n-1}+\cdots+a_{n-1}xD+a_n)y=X, \quad D=\frac{d}{dx}$$

where $a_0, a_1, a_2, \ldots, a_n$ are constants, and X is either a constant or a function of x only, is called a homogeneous linear differential equation. In such equations, the index of x and the order of the derivative are the same in each term. These equations are also referred to as Cauchy-Euler equations.

3.2.2 Homogeneous Linear Differential Equation

$$(a_0x^nD^n+a_1x^{n-1}D^{n-1}+\cdots+a_{n-1}xD+a_n)y=X$$

In order to solve the above equation, introduce a new independent variable z such that

$$x=e^z \quad \text{or} \quad \log x=z, \quad \text{so that} \quad \frac{1}{x}=\frac{dz}{dx}.$$

Now,

$$\frac{dy}{dx}=\frac{dy}{dz}\cdot\frac{dz}{dx}=\frac{1}{x}\frac{dy}{dz}.$$

Again,

$$\frac{d^2y}{dx^2}=\frac{d}{dx}\left(\frac{dy}{dx}\right)=\frac{d}{dz}\left(\frac{dy}{dz}\cdot\frac{1}{x}\right)=\frac{1}{x^2}\frac{d^2y}{dz^2}$$

and so on. Proceeding likewise, we can show that

$$x^nD^n=(D_1(D_1-1)(D_1-2)\ldots(D_1-n+1))\,y.$$

Substituting the above values of $x, xD, x^2D^2, x^3D^3, \ldots, x^nD^n$ in (1) and thus changing the independent variable from x to z, we have

$$[a_0D_1(D_1-1)\ldots(D_1-n+1)+\cdots+a_{n-2}D_1(D_1-1)+a_{n-1}D_1+a_n]y=Z,$$

or equivalently,

$$f(D_1)y = Z,$$

where Z is now a function of z only.

3.2.3 Working Rule

Step I: Put $x = e^z$ or $z = \log x$, where $x > 0$.
Step II: Assume that $D_1 = \frac{d}{dz}$ and $D = \frac{d}{dx}$. Then, we have

$$xD = D_1, \quad x^2D^2 = D_1(D_1 - 1), \quad x^3D^3 = D_1(D_1 - 1)(D_1 - 2), \quad \dots$$

Then equation (1) reduces to

$$f(D_1)y = Z, \quad \text{where } Z \text{ is now a function of } z \text{ only.}$$

Step III: The general solution $y = g(z)$.

Since $z = \log x$, the desired solution is

$$y = g(\log x), \quad x > 0.$$

Note: While solving any equation, remember that $e^{m \log n} = n^m$.
Example: Solve $x^2y'' + xy' - 4y = 0$

$$(x^2D^2 + xD - 4)y = 0, \quad \text{where } D = \frac{d}{dx}.$$

Let $x = e^z$ (or $z = \log x$) and $D_1 = \frac{d}{dz}$, so that $xD = D_1$ and $x^2D^2 = D_1(D_1 - 1)$.

$$[D_1(D_1 - 1) + D_1 - 4]y = 0 \quad \text{or} \quad (D_1^2 - 4)y = 0.$$

The auxiliary equation is

$$D_1^2 - 4 = 0 \quad \Rightarrow \quad D_1 = 2, -2.$$

Hence, the general solution is

$$y = c_1 e^{2z} + c_2 e^{-2z} = c_1 e^{2\log x} + c_2 e^{-2\log x} = c_1 x^2 + c_2 x^{-2},$$

as $z = \log x$, where c_1 and c_2 are arbitrary constants.

Solve

- $x^2 y'' + xy' + 4y = 0; x > 0$ with $y(1) = 0$ and $y(e^{\frac{\pi}{2}}) = 1$.
- $x^2 y'' + xy' + y = 0; x > 0$ with $y(1) = 0$ and $y(e^{\frac{\pi}{2}}) = 1$.

3.3 Higher-Order Differential Equations

Higher-order differential equations can be expressed as:

$$a_n y^{(n)} + a_{n-1} y^{(n-1)} + ... + a_1 y' + a_0 y = f(x)$$

The methods for solving higher-order equations are similar to those for second-order equations but involve more complex characteristic polynomials.

Example: Solve $y''' - y'' - y' + y = e^{-x}$

1. Find the complementary function by solving the characteristic polynomial. The characteristic polynomial is:

$$r^3 - r^2 - r + 1 = 0$$

Using synthetic division or factoring gives us roots.

3.4 Conclusion

This chapter has provided an overview of second-order and higher-order differential equations, including methods for solving both homogeneous and non-homogeneous cases with constant and variable coefficients. Techniques such as finding complementary functions and particular integrals have been discussed in detail, supported by examples illustrating each method's application.

Chapter 4

The Wronskian and Its Applications in Differential Equations

Nature is written in the language of mathematics, and differential equations are its syntax.

— Galileo Galile

The Wronskian is a determinant used in the study of differential equations, particularly in determining the linear independence of solutions to linear differential equations. Named after the Polish mathematician Józef Hoene-Wroński, the Wronskian provides valuable insights into the behavior of solutions and is essential for constructing general solutions to linear differential equations.

- **Higher Order Linear Differential Equations** Consider n^{th} order linear differential equation:

  $$a_0(x)y^n + a_1(x)y^{n-1} + ... + a_{n-1}y' + a_n(x)y = Q(x) \;\; \forall x \in [a, b]$$

  where $a_0(x) \neq 0; a_1(x), a_2(x), ..., a_n(x), Q(x)$ are continuous $\forall x \in [a, b]$.

- **Second Order Linear Differential Equations**

  $$a_0(x)y'' + a_1(x)y' + a_2(x)y = 0 \;\; \forall x \in [a, b]$$

  where $a_0(x) \neq 0; a_1(x), a_2(x)$ are continuous $\forall x \in [a, b]$.

4.1 Definition of the Wronskian

Let y_1 & y_2 be two solutions of $y'' + p(x)y' + q(x)y = 0$ on $[a, b]$. Let $y(x) = c_1y_1 + c_2y_2$ be the general solution c_1 & c_2 are arbitrary constants.
Let $x_0 \in [a, b]$

$$\begin{aligned} c_1y_1(x_0) + c_2y_2(x_0) &= y(x_0) \\ c_1y_1'(x_0) + c_2y_2'(x_0) &= y'(x_0) \end{aligned}$$

To find c_1 and c_2

$$\begin{bmatrix} y_1(x_0) & y_2(x_0) \\ y_1'(x_0) & y_2'(x_0) \end{bmatrix} \begin{bmatrix} c_1 \\ c_2 \end{bmatrix} = \begin{bmatrix} y(x_0) \\ y'(x_0) \end{bmatrix}$$

This system has a unique solution if $y_1(x_0)y_2'(x_0) - y_2(x_0)y_1'(x_0) \neq 0$ and

$$W(y_1, y_2)(x_0) = W = y_1(x_0)y_2'(x_0) - y_2(x_0)y_1'(x_0)$$

is known as the Wronskian of $y_1 \& y_2$.

For a set of n differentiable functions $y_1, y_2, \ldots, y_n$, the Wronskian $W(y_1, y_2, \ldots, y_n)$ is defined as the determinant of the following matrix:

$$W(y_1, y_2, \ldots, y_n) = \begin{vmatrix} y_1 & y_2 & \cdots & y_n \\ y_1' & y_2' & \cdots & y_n' \\ \vdots & \vdots & \ddots & \vdots \\ y_1^{(n-1)} & y_2^{(n-1)} & \cdots & y_n^{(n-1)} \end{vmatrix}$$

where $y_i^{(k)}$ denotes the k-th derivative of y_i.

4.2 Linear Combinations and Solutions

4.2.1 Linear Combinations

A linear combination of functions involves creating new functions by multiplying existing functions by constants and adding them together. For example, if we have two functions y_1 and y_2, a linear combination can be expressed as:

$$y = C_1y_1 + C_2y_2$$

where C_1 and C_2 are constants.

4.2.2 Dependent and Independent Solutions

- Linearly Independent Solutions: Two functions y_1 and y_2 are said to be linearly independent if there are no constants C_1 and C_2, not both zero, such that:

$$C_1y_1 + C_2y_2 = 0$$

If their Wronskian is non-zero at some point in their domain, they are linearly independent.

- Linearly Dependent Solutions: Conversely, if there exist constants C_1 and C_2, not both zero, such that:

$$C_1y_1 + C_2y_2 = 0$$

then y_1 and y_2 are linearly dependent.

4.2.3 Linearly dependent and independent set of functions

Functions $y_1(x), y_2(x), ..., y_n(x)$ are linearly dependent if there exist constants $c_1, c_2, ..., c_n$ (not all zero), such that

$$c_1y_1 + c_2y_2 + ... + c_ny_n = 0$$

If $c_1 = c_2 = ... = c_n = 0$, then $y_1, y_2, ..., y_n$ are said to be linearly independent.

- Let y_1 and y_2 are any two solution of homogeneous linear differential equation on $[a, b]$ then every linear combination of the solution is also a solution.

- In general every n^{th} order homogeneous linear differential equation has exactly n linearly independent solution.

- Every n^{th} order non-homogeneous linear differential equation has exactly $n + 1$ linearly independent solution (as Particular integral is also LI to other solution).

- **Principal of Superposition:** If differential equation is homogeneous then every linear combination of solution is also solution but in case of non-homogeneous equation sum of coefficient should be 1.

4.3 Abel-Liouville Formula

Consider

$$a_0(x)y'' + a_1(x)y' + a_2(x)y = 0 \;\; \forall x \in [a, b]$$

where $a_0(x) \neq 0; a_1(x), a_2(x)$ are continuous $\forall x \in [a, b]$, then

$$W(x) = ce^{-\int \frac{a_1(x)}{a_0(x)} dx}$$

Let y_1 and y_2 are two solution. Then,

$$\begin{aligned} a_0(x)y_1'' + a_1(x)y_1' + a_2(x)y_1 = 0 \\ a_0(x)y_2'' + a_1(x)y_2' + a_2(x)y_2 = 0 \end{aligned}$$

$\implies a_0(x)(y_1y_2'' - y_2y_1'') + a_1(x)(y_1y_2' - y_2y_1') = 0$ and

$$W(y_1, y_2)(x) = \begin{vmatrix} y_1 & y_2 \\ y_1' & y_2' \end{vmatrix} = y_1y_2' - y_2y_1'$$

$$W'(y_1, y_2)(x) = \begin{vmatrix} y_1 & y_2 \\ y_1'' & y_2'' \end{vmatrix} = y_1 y_2'' - y_2 y_1''$$

$$\implies a_0(x)W' + a_1(x)W = 0$$

$$W(x) = ce^{-\int \frac{a_1(x)}{a_0(x)}dx} \text{ provided } a_0(x) \neq 0$$

Let $W(x) = ce^{-F(x)}$ and $W(x_0) = ce^{-F(x_0)} = \alpha \implies W(x) = \alpha c e^{F(x_0)} e^{-F(x)}$

- If $\alpha = 0 \implies W(x) = 0 \,\forall\, x$
- If $\alpha > 0 \implies W(x) > 0 \,\forall x$.
- If $\alpha < 0 \implies W(x) < 0 \,\forall\, x$.

The Abel-Liouville formula provides a relationship between the Wronskian of solutions to a linear differential equation and its coefficients. For a second-order linear homogeneous differential equation given by

$$y'' + p(t)y' + q(t)y = 0,$$

the formula states that if $W(y_1, y_2)$ is the Wronskian of two solutions y_1 and y_2 then:

$$W(y_1, y_2)(t) = Ce^{-\int p(t)dt},$$

where C is a constant determined by initial conditions.

Example Given the equation

$$y'' - 3y' + 3y = 0,$$

$$p(t) = -3.$$

Using Abel's formula,

$$W(y_1, y_2)(t) = Ce^{-(-3)t} = Ce^{3t}.$$

This relationship allows us to compute or verify solutions based on known properties of their Wronskian.

4.4 Properties of Wronskian

1. - Let $y_1 \& y_2$ are two solution of homogeneous D.E. then $W = W(y_1, y_2)$ is either identically zero or never zero.
   - Let $y_1 \& y_2$ are two solution of homogeneous D.E. then they are LD iff their wronskian is identically zero.
   - Let $y_1 \& y_2$ are two solution of homogeneous D.E. then they are LI iff their wronskian is never zero.
   - Wronskian never changes its sign.
   - For any n^{th} order D.E. the first derivative of the wronskian of any n solution is always exists but higher order derivative may or may not exists.

2. The solution of homogeneous L.D.E. are linearly dependent if
   - They have common zero x_0 in the interval.
   - They have maximum and minimum at the same point x_0 in the interval (common point of extrima).
   - x_0 is repeated zero either of y_1 or y_2.

3. Let solution of homogeneous L.D.E. are linearly independent then
   - They does not have common zero x_0 in the interval.
   - They does not have maximum and minimum at the same point x_0 in the interval (common point of extrima).
   - They does not is repeated zero either of y_1 or y_2.

4. Let y_1 and y_2 are two linearly independent solution of the D.E.

$$a_0(x)y'' + a_1(x)y' + a_2(x)y = 0 \;\; \forall x \in [a, b]$$

   where $a_0(x) \neq 0; a_1(x), a_2(x)$ are continuous $\forall x \in [a, b]$.
   If $y(x) = \dfrac{y_1(x)}{y_2(x)}$; where $y_2(x) \neq 0 \; \forall \; x \in [a, b]$ then $y(x)$ is monotonic function.

- If $W(x) > 0$ then $y(x)$ is strictly decreasing.
- If $W(x) < 0$ then $y(x)$ is strictly increasing.

5. Let y_1 and y_2 are two linearly independent solution of the D.E. then $ay_1 + by_2$ and $cy_1 + dy_2$ is also linearly independent if $ad - bc \neq 0$.

6. Let $\{y_1, y_2\}$ be the set of LI solution of given D.E. and $\{g_1, g_2\}$ be the another set of LI solution of the given D.E. then

$$W(g_1, g_2)(x) = DW(y_1, y_2)(x)$$

where D is non zero constant. Consider LDE $a_0(x)y''+a_1(x)y'+a_2(x)y = 0 \ \forall x \in \mathbb{R}$ where $a_0(x) \neq 0; a_1(x), a_2(x)$ are continuous $\forall x \in \mathbb{R}$.

7. Let $y(x)$ be non-trivial solution of the D.E. If $A = \{\alpha \in \mathbb{R} : y(\alpha) = 0\}$ then

    - A does not have ant limit point
    - Every $x_0 \in A$ is isolated point
    - A is always countable.
    - A cannot be bounded and infinite.
    - A is bounded iff it is finite

8. Let y_1 and y_2 are two linearly independent solution of the DE. If $A = \{\alpha \in \mathbb{R} : y_1(\alpha) = 0\}$ and $B = \{\beta \in \mathbb{R} : y_2(\beta) = 0\}$ then

    - $A \cap B = \phi$
    - If $\alpha_0 < \alpha_1 \in A \ \exists \ \beta_0 \in B$ such that $\alpha_0 < \beta_0 < \alpha_1$ i.e. between two successive zeroes of y_1 there must exists exactly one zero of y_2 and conversely.
    - A and B must be nowhere dense in $\mathbb{R}$
    - A is bounded iff B is bounded.
    - A is bounded iff B is finite.
    - A is finite iff B is finite.

4.5 Applications of the Wronskian

4.5.1 Determining Linear Independence

The primary application of the Wronskian is to determine whether a set of solutions to a differential equation is linearly independent. For example, consider the second-order linear homogeneous differential equation:

$$y'' + p(t)y' + q(t)y = 0$$

Suppose we have two solutions $y_1(t)$ and $y_2(t)$. To check if these solutions are linearly independent, we compute their Wronskian:

$$W(y_1, y_2)(t) = \begin{vmatrix} y_1(t) & y_2(t) \\ y_1'(t) & y_2'(t) \end{vmatrix} = y_1(t)y_2'(t) - y_2(t)y_1'(t)$$

If $W(y_1, y_2)(t) \neq 0$, then y_1 and y_2 are linearly independent.

4.5.2 Fundamental Set of Solutions

In solving higher-order linear differential equations, finding a fundamental set of solutions is crucial. A fundamental set consists of n linearly independent solutions to an nth-order linear homogeneous differential equation. For example:

$$y'' - 3y' + 2y = 0$$

The characteristic equation is:

$$r^2 - 3r + 2 = 0$$

Factoring gives us roots $r = 1$ and $r = 2$, leading to two solutions:

$$y_1(t) = e^t$$

$$y_2(t) = e^{2t}$$

To confirm that these form a fundamental set:

Calculate their Wronskian:

$$W(y_1, y_2)(t) = \begin{vmatrix} e^t & e^{2t} \\ e^t & 2e^{2t} \end{vmatrix} = e^t(2e^{2t}) - e^{2t}(e^t) = 2e^{3t} - e^{3t} = e^{3t}$$

Since this is non-zero for all t, we confirm that they form a fundamental set.

4.6 Conclusion

The Wronskian serves as a powerful tool in solving linear differential equations by providing a straightforward method for determining linear independence among solutions. Its applications extend beyond mere verification; it plays a critical role in constructing general solutions and understanding the behavior of systems modeled by differential equations. Mastering the concept of the Wronskian equips students and practitioners with essential skills for tackling complex mathematical problems effectively.

Chapter 5

Sturm-Liouville Boundary Value Problems

Eigenfunctions and eigenvalues are the heart of many physical and mathematical problems.
— David C. Lay

The Sturm-Liouville boundary value problem (SLBVP) is a pivotal topic in differential equations, especially in areas like mathematical physics and engineering. It involves determining the eigenvalues and eigenfunctions for a second-order linear differential operator within a specified interval, subject to boundary conditions. A key tool in this analysis is the Wronskian, which helps in assessing the linear independence of the solutions.

5.1 Adjoint Equation

Consider the second-order homogeneous linear differential equation (L.D.E.):

$$a_0(x)y''(x) + a_1(x)y'(x) + a_2(x)y(x) = 0 \quad \text{for } x \in [a, b], \tag{5.1.1}$$

where $a_0(x)$ has a continuous second derivative, $a_1(x)$ has a continuous first derivative, and $a_2(x)$ is continuous with $a_0(x) \neq 0$ for all $x \in [a, b]$. The corresponding adjoint equation is:

$$\frac{d^2}{dx^2}(a_0(x)y) - \frac{d}{dx}(a_1(x)y) + a_2(x)y = 0. \tag{5.1.2}$$

This simplifies to:

$$a_0(x)y'' + (2a_0'(x) - a_1(x))y' + (a_0''(x) - a_1'(x) + a_2(x))y = 0. \tag{5.1.3}$$

Self-Adjoint Equation: The equation is termed *self-adjoint* if it is identical to its adjoint equation. In this case, the following condition holds:

$$2a_0'(x) - a_1(x) = a_1(x) \quad \Rightarrow \quad a_0'(x) = a_1(x).$$

Important Notes:

- The necessary and sufficient condition for the differential equation to be self-adjoint is $a_0'(x) = a_1(x)$.
- If the second-order homogeneous linear differential equation $a_0(x)y''(x) + a_1(x)y'(x) + a_2(x)y(x) = 0$ is self-adjoint, it can be expressed as:

$$\frac{d}{dx}(a_0(x)y') + a_2(x)y = 0.$$

- If the equation is not self-adjoint, it can be converted into a self-adjoint form by multiplying through by $\frac{1}{a_0(x)}e^{\int \frac{a_1(x)}{a_0(x)}dx}$.

Example: Find the adjoint equation for the differential equation $x^2y'' + 7xy' + 8y = 0$.

Theorem 5.1.1 (Limit Points and the Bolzano-Weierstrass Theorem)**.** *Let E be a set of points on the t-axis. A point t_0 is said to be a limit point of E if there exists a sequence of distinct points $t_1, t_2, t_3, \ldots$ from E such that:*

$$\lim_{n\to\infty} t_n = t_0.$$

The Bolzano-Weierstrass Theorem states that every bounded infinite set E has at least one limit point.

Theorem 5.1.2 (Uniqueness of Solution to Homogeneous Equations)**.** *If ϕ is a solution to the homogeneous differential equation:*

$$a_0(t)\frac{d^n x}{dt^n} + a_1(t)\frac{d^{n-1}x}{dt^{n-1}} + \cdots + a_n(t)x = 0,$$

and satisfies $\phi(t_0) = 0$, $\phi'(t_0) = 0$, ..., $\phi^{(n-1)}(t_0) = 0$, for some t_0 in the interval $[a, b]$, where the coefficients $a_0(t), a_1(t), \ldots, a_n(t)$ are continuous and $a_0(t) \neq 0$, then $\phi(t) = 0$ for all $t \in [a, b]$.

Theorem 5.1.3 (Linear Dependence and the Wronskian)**.** *Let $f_1, f_2, \ldots, f_n$ be solutions to the homogeneous linear differential equation:*

$$a_0(t)\frac{d^n x}{dt^n} + a_1(t)\frac{d^{n-1}x}{dt^{n-1}} + \cdots + a_n(t)x = 0.$$

These solutions are linearly dependent on the interval $[a, b]$ if and only if their Wronskian is zero for all $t \in [a, b]$, i.e.:

$$W(f_1, f_2, \ldots, f_n)(t) = 0 \quad \textit{for all } t \in [a, b],$$

where $W(f_1, f_2, \ldots, f_n)(t)$ denotes the Wronskian of the solutions $f_1, f_2, \ldots, f_n$ at t.

5.2 Sturm's Theorem

Theorem 5.2.1. *Let f be a solution to the equation*

$$\frac{d}{dt}\left(P(t)\frac{dx}{dt}\right) + Q(t)x = 0,$$

where f' is the first derivative of f over the interval $a \leq t \leq b$, and assume that f has an infinite number of zeros in the interval $[a, b]$.
Conclusion: *In this case, $f(t) = 0$ for all $t \in [a, b]$.*

Proof. Since f has infinitely many zeros within $[a, b]$, by the Bolzano-Weierstrass theorem, the set of zeros must contain a limit point $t_0 \in [a, b]$. Therefore, there exists a sequence $\{t_n\}$ of zeros of f that converges to t_0 (with $t_n \neq t_0$). Since f is continuous, we can write

$$\lim_{t \to t_0} f(t) = f(t_0),$$

where $t \to t_0$ through any sequence of points in $[a, b]$. Choosing $t \to t_0$ via the sequence of zeros $\{t_n\}$, we obtain

$$\lim_{t \to t_0} f(t) = 0 = f(t_0).$$

Now, since $f'(t_0)$ exists, we have

$$f'(t_0) = \lim_{t \to t_0} \frac{f(t) - f(t_0)}{t - t_0},$$

where $t \to t_0$ via the sequence $\{t_n\}$. For these points, we find that

$$f(t) - f(t_0) = 0,$$

implying that $f'(t_0) = 0$. Therefore, f satisfies the condition that $f(t_0) = f'(t_0) = 0$. Hence, we conclude that $f(t) = 0$ for all $t \in [a, b]$. □

5.3 Abel's Formula

Theorem 5.3.1. ***Hypothesis:*** *Let f and g be two solutions of the differential equation*

$$\frac{d}{dt}\left(P(t)\frac{dx}{dt}\right) + Q(t)x = 0,$$

on the interval $a \leq t \leq b$.
Conclusion: *Then, for all t in $[a, b]$,*

$$P(t)[f(t)g'(t) - f'(t)g(t)] = k,$$

where k is a constant.

Proof. Since f and g are solutions on $[a,b]$, we have the following equations:

$$\frac{d}{dt}\left[P(t)f'(t)\right]+Q(t)f(t)=0 \quad \text{and} \quad \frac{d}{dt}\left[P(t)g'(t)\right]+Q(t)g(t)=0$$

for all $t \in [a,b]$. Multiply the first equation by $-g(t)$ and the second by $f(t)$, and then add them together:

$$f(t)\frac{d}{dt}\left[P(t)g'(t)\right]-g(t)\frac{d}{dt}\left[P(t)f'(t)\right]=0.$$

On integrating both sides, we get

$$P(t)[f(t)g'(t)-f'(t)g(t)]=P(a)[f(a)g'(a)-f'(a)g(a)]=k \quad \text{(constant)}.$$

Thus, we obtain Abel's formula. □

Theorem 5.3.2. *Let f and g be two solutions of the equation*

$$\frac{d}{dt}\left(P(t)\frac{dx}{dt}+Q(t)x\right)=0,$$

such that f and g share a common zero on the interval $a \le t \le b$.
Conclusion: *Then f and g are linearly dependent on $[a,b]$.*

Proof. By Abel's formula, we have

$$P(t)[f(t)g'(t)-f'(t)g(t)]=k.$$

Let $t_0 \in [a,b]$ be the common zero of f and g, so that $f(t_0)=g(t_0)=0$. Substituting $t=t_0$ into Abel's formula, we obtain $k=0$. Therefore, we have

$$P(t)[f(t)g'(t)-f'(t)g(t)]=0 \quad \text{for all } t \in [a,b].$$

Since we assume that $P(t) \neq 0$ on $[a,b]$, it follows that

$$f(t)g'(t)-f'(t)g(t)=0 \quad \text{for all } t \in [a,b].$$

This quantity is the Wronskian $W(f, g)(t)$, so we conclude that the solutions f and g are linearly dependent on $[a, b]$. □

Theorem 5.3.3. *Let f and g be nontrivial, linearly dependent solutions on $[a, b]$, and suppose that $f(t_0) = 0$, where t_0 is such that $a \leq t_0 \leq b$.*
Conclusion: *Then $g(t_0) = 0$.*

Proof. Since f and g are linearly dependent on $[a, b]$, there exist constants c_1 and c_2 (not both zero) such that

$$c_1 f(t) + c_2 g(t) = 0,$$

for all $t \in [a, b]$. Since neither f nor g is identically zero on $[a, b]$, if $c_1 = 0$, we would have $c_2 g(t) = 0$ for all $t \in [a, b]$. Since $g(t)$ is not identically zero, we must have $c_2 = 0$, which is a contradiction. Thus, $c_1 \neq 0$ and $c_2 \neq 0$. Therefore, since $f(t_0) = 0$, substituting $t = t_0$ into the equation yields $c_2 g(t_0) = 0$, implying that $g(t_0) = 0$. □

Example

Consider the equation

$$\frac{d^2x}{dt^2} + x = 0,$$

where $P(t) = Q(t) = 1$ on every interval $a \leq t \leq b$. The linearly dependent solutions are $A\sin(t)$ and $B\sin(t)$, which share the common zeros $t = \pm n\pi$ ($n = 0, 1, 2, \ldots$) and no other zeros.

5.4 Sturm Separation Theorem

Theorem 5.4.1. *Let f and g be real linearly independent solutions of the differential equation*

$$\frac{d}{dt}\left(P(t)\frac{dx}{dt}\right) + Q(t)x = 0$$

on the interval $a \leq t \leq b$.
Conclusion: *Between any two consecutive zeros of f (or g), there is precisely one zero of g (or f).*

Proof. Let t_1 and t_2 be two consecutive zeros of f on $[a, b]$. Then, $g(t_1) \neq 0$ and $g(t_2) \neq 0$. Assume that g has no zero in the open interval $t_1 < t < t_2$.

Since the solutions f and g have continuous derivatives on $[a, b]$, the quotient $\frac{f(t)}{g(t)}$ has a continuous derivative on the interval $t_1 \leq t \leq t_2$. Further, $\frac{f(t)}{g(t)}$ is zero at the endpoints of this interval. By Rolle's theorem, there exists ξ, where $t_1 < \xi < t_2$, such that

$$\frac{d}{dt}\left(\frac{f(t)}{g(t)}\right)_{t=\xi} = 0.$$

But

$$\frac{d}{dt}\left(\frac{f(t)}{g(t)}\right) = \frac{W(g, f)(t)}{g(t)^2},$$

where $W(g, f)(t)$ is the Wronskian of f and g. Since f and g are linearly independent on $[a, b]$, we have $W(f, g)(t) \neq 0$ on $t_1 < t < t_2$, implying that

$$\frac{d}{dt}\left(\frac{f(t)}{g(t)}\right) \neq 0 \quad \text{on} \quad t_1 < t < t_2.$$

This contradicts the assumption that the derivative is zero at some point. Thus, g must have at least one zero in the interval $t_1 < t < t_2$.

Now suppose g has more than one zero in $t_1 < t < t_2$. Let t_3 and t_4 be two consecutive zeros of g. By interchanging f and g and applying the same reasoning, we can show that f must have at least one zero in the interval $t_3 < t < t_4$. This implies that there exists a zero t_5 of f such that $t_1 < t_5 < t_2$, contradicting the assumption that t_1 and t_2 are consecutive zeros of f. Therefore, g has exactly one zero in the open interval $t_1 < t < t_2$.

Conclusion: The zeros of one of two real linearly independent solutions separate the zeros of the other solution. □

Example:

We have already observed that the equation

$$\frac{d^2x}{dt^2} + x = 0$$

has solutions $f(t) = \sin t$ and $g(t) = \cos t$. These two functions are linearly independent solutions of this equation. Between any two consecutive zeros of one of these solutions, there is precisely one zero of the other solution.

We know that the zeros of $f(t)$ are given by $t = n\pi$ where $n = 0, \pm 1, \pm 2, \ldots$, and the zeros of $g(t)$ are given by $t = (2n+1)\frac{\pi}{2}$ where $n = 0, 1, 2, \ldots$. The zeros of $f(t)$ and $g(t)$ are separated by each other, as stated in the theorem.

5.5 Sturm's Fundamental Comparison Theorem

Theorem 5.5.1. *Let ϕ_1 and ϕ_2 be two real solutions of the following second-order linear differential equations on the interval $a \le t \le b$:*

$$\frac{d}{dt}\left(P(t)\frac{dx}{dt}\right) + Q_1(t)x = 0,$$

$$\frac{d}{dt}\left(P(t)\frac{dx}{dt}\right) + Q_2(t)x = 0,$$

where $P(t)$ is a continuously differentiable function with $P(t) > 0$, and $Q_1(t)$ and $Q_2(t)$ are continuous functions such that $Q_2(t) > Q_1(t)$ for all $t \in [a, b]$. If t_1 and t_2 are consecutive zeros of ϕ_1, then ϕ_2 must have at least one zero in the open interval $t_1 < t < t_2$.

Proof. Assume, for contradiction, that ϕ_2 has no zeros in the open interval $t_1 < t < t_2$, and without loss of generality, assume that both $\phi_1(t)$ and $\phi_2(t)$ are positive in this interval. By the given conditions, we have the following equations for all $t \in [a, b]$:

$$\frac{d}{dt}\left(P(t)\frac{d\phi_1}{dt}\right) + Q_1(t)\phi_1 = 0,$$

$$\frac{d}{dt}\left(P(t)\frac{d\phi_2}{dt}\right) + Q_2(t)\phi_2 = 0.$$

Multiplying the first equation by $\phi_2(t)$ and the second by $\phi_1(t)$, and then subtracting them, we obtain:

$$\frac{d}{dt}\left[P(t)(\phi_1'(t)\phi_2(t) - \phi_1(t)\phi_2'(t))\right] = (Q_2(t) - Q_1(t))\phi_1(t)\phi_2(t).$$

Integrating both sides from t_1 to t_2, we have:

$$\int_{t_1}^{t_2} (Q_2(t) - Q_1(t))\phi_1(t)\phi_2(t)\,dt = \left[P(t)(\phi_1'(t)\phi_2(t) - \phi_1(t)\phi_2'(t))\right]_{t_1}^{t_2}.$$

Since $\phi_1(t_1) = \phi_1(t_2) = 0$, this simplifies to:

$$\int_{t_1}^{t_2} (Q_2(t) - Q_1(t))\phi_1(t)\phi_2(t)\,dt = P(t_2)\phi_1'(t_2)\phi_2(t_2) - P(t_1)\phi_1'(t_1)\phi_2(t_1).$$

By the assumption that $P(t_2) > 0$ and $\phi_1(t_2) = 0$, we deduce that $\phi_1'(t_2) < 0$. Therefore, the left-hand side is non-positive, whereas the right-hand side, due to $Q_2(t) - Q_1(t) > 0$, is positive. This contradiction shows that our assumption that ϕ_2 has no zeros in the interval is false. Hence, ϕ_2 must have at least one zero in the open interval $t_1 < t < t_2$.

□

Example

Consider the equations:

$$\frac{d^2x}{dt^2} + A^2x = 0,$$

$$\frac{d^2x}{dt^2} + B^2x = 0,$$

where A and B are constants with $B > A > 0$. The solutions $\phi_1(t) = \sin(At)$ and $\phi_2(t) = \sin(Bt)$ are real solutions to these equations. The zeros of $\sin(At)$ occur at $t_n = \frac{n\pi}{A}$ for $n = 0, 1, 2, \ldots$. By applying the theorem, we conclude that the zeros of $\sin(Bt)$ lie in the intervals between consecutive zeros of $\sin(At)$. Specifically, for $n = 0$, the zero of $\sin(At)$ is $t_1 = 0$, and the next zero is $t_2 = \frac{\pi}{A}$, while the next zero of $\sin(Bt)$ is $\xi_1 = \frac{\pi}{B}$. Since $B > A$, we have $\frac{\pi}{B} < \frac{\pi}{A}$, verifying the result of the comparison theorem.

5.6 Boundary Value Problems (BVP)

- Boundary value problems are defined as those that combine a differential equation with additional constraints, which the solution of the differential equation must adhere to.
- When all the given constraints are specified at a single x-value, it is referred to as an initial-value problem (or a one-point boundary value problem).
- On the other hand, when the constraints are provided at two distinct x-values, it is termed a two-point boundary value problem (commonly known as a boundary value problem).

Example

$$\frac{d^2y}{dx^2} + y = 0, \quad y(1) = 3, \quad y'(1) = -4.$$

$$\frac{d^2y}{dx^2} + y = 0, \quad y(0) = 1, \quad y\left(\frac{\pi}{2}\right) = 5.$$

In this scenario, we seek a solution to the same differential equation, but the solution is required to satisfy the condition that its value is 1 at $x = 0$ and 5 at $x = \frac{\pi}{2}$. Since these conditions are specified at two distinct values of x, it represents a (two-point) boundary value problem with a unique solution.

5.7 Sturm-Liouville Equation

- The classical Sturm-Liouville equation, named after Jacques Charles François Sturm (1803–1855) and Joseph Liouville (1809–1882), is a second-order linear differential equation expressed as:

  $$\frac{d}{dx}\left(p(x)\frac{dy}{dx}\right) + [q(x) + \lambda r(x)]y = 0,$$

  where y is a function dependent on the variable x.
- In this equation, the function $p(x) > 0$ has a continuous derivative, while $q(x)$ and $r(x) > 0$ are predefined functions that are continuous over a finite closed interval $[a, b]$ in the simplest cases.

- The function $r(x)$ is referred to as the "weight" or "density" function.
- The parameter λ is not explicitly given in the equation. Identifying the values of λ for which non-trivial solutions exist that satisfy the boundary conditions is part of the Sturm-Liouville problem (SL).
- These specific values of λ, if they exist, are termed eigenvalues of the boundary value problem defined by the equation and the given boundary conditions. The corresponding solutions associated with these eigenvalues are known as the eigenfunctions of the problem.

5.8 Sturm-Liouville Boundary Value Problems (SLBVP)

A Sturm-Liouville boundary value problem consists of the following components:

- A second-order homogeneous linear differential equation given by

$$\frac{d}{dx}\left(p(x)\frac{dy}{dx}\right) + [q(x) + \lambda r(x)]y = 0,$$

  where p, q, and r are real-valued functions. The function p has a continuous derivative, q and r are continuous, and $p(x) > 0$ as well as $r(x) > 0$ for all x in the interval $a \leq x \leq b$. Here, λ is a parameter that does not depend on x.

- Two additional boundary conditions are specified as follows:

$$A_1 y(a) + A_2 y'(a) = 0,$$
$$B_1 y(b) + B_2 y'(b) = 0,$$

  where A_1, A_2, B_1, and B_2 are real constants. For the conditions to be valid, A_1 and A_2 cannot both be zero, and similarly, B_1 and B_2 cannot both be zero.

Such a boundary value problem is referred to as a Sturm-Liouville problem or Sturm-Liouville system.

Example Determine the nontrivial solutions of the Sturm-Liouville problem

$$\frac{d^2y}{dx^2} + \lambda y = 0,$$

with boundary conditions

$$y(0) = 0, \quad y(\pi) = 0.$$

Solution Let us analyze the problem for the three cases: $\lambda = 0$, $\lambda < 0$, and $\lambda > 0$. In each scenario, we first derive the general solution of the differential equation, then impose the boundary conditions to determine the constants.

Case 1: $\lambda = 0$
For $\lambda = 0$, the differential equation becomes

$$\frac{d^2y}{dx^2} = 0.$$

The general solution is

$$y = c_1 + c_2 x.$$

Using the boundary conditions $y(0) = 0$ and $y(\pi) = 0$, we find $c_1 = 0$ and $c_2 = 0$, resulting in the trivial solution $y(x) = 0$. Thus, no nontrivial solution exists for $\lambda = 0$.

Case 2: $\lambda < 0$
When $\lambda < 0$, the differential equation's characteristic equation is $m^2 + \lambda = 0$, leading to roots $\pm\sqrt{-\lambda}$, which are real and distinct. Let $\sqrt{-\lambda} = \alpha$. The general solution is

$$y = c_1 e^{\alpha x} + c_2 e^{-\alpha x}.$$

Imposing $y(0) = 0$, we get $c_1 + c_2 = 0$. Substituting $y(\pi) = 0$ gives

$$c_1 e^{\alpha \pi} + c_2 e^{-\alpha \pi} = 0.$$

This leads to $e^{\alpha\pi} = e^{-\alpha\pi}$, implying $\alpha = 0$, which contradicts $\lambda < 0$. Therefore, no nontrivial solutions exist for $\lambda < 0$.

Case 3: $\lambda > 0$

For $\lambda > 0$, the roots of the characteristic equation are complex conjugates $\pm i\sqrt{\lambda}$. The general solution is

$$y = c_1 \sin(\sqrt{\lambda}x) + c_2 \cos(\sqrt{\lambda}x).$$

Using $y(0) = 0$, we find $c_2 = 0$. Imposing $y(\pi) = 0$ gives

$$c_1 \sin(\sqrt{\lambda}\pi) = 0.$$

To avoid the trivial solution ($c_1 = 0$), we require $\sin(\sqrt{\lambda}\pi) = 0$, which occurs if $\sqrt{\lambda}\pi = n\pi$ for $n = 1, 2, 3, \ldots$. Thus,

$$\lambda = n^2, \quad n = 1, 2, 3, \ldots.$$

Conclusion: Nontrivial solutions exist only if $\lambda > 0$ and $\lambda = n^2$ for $n = 1, 2, 3, \ldots$. The eigenfunctions corresponding to these eigenvalues are

$$y = c_n \sin(nx), \quad n = 1, 2, 3, \ldots,$$

where c_n are arbitrary nonzero constants. The solutions are therefore given by the functions $c_1 \sin x, c_2 \sin 2x, c_3 \sin 3x, \ldots$, where $c_1, c_2, c_3, \ldots$ are nonzero constants.

Example Find the nontrivial solutions of the Sturm-Liouville problem

$$\frac{d^2y}{dx^2} + \lambda y = 0,$$

with boundary conditions

$$y(0) = y(\pi), \quad y'(0) = y'(\pi).$$

Solution We consider three cases: $\lambda = 0$, $\lambda < 0$, and $\lambda > 0$. In each case, we first solve the differential equation and then apply the boundary conditions to determine the constants.

Case 1: $\lambda = 0$ In this case, the differential equation becomes

$$\frac{d^2y}{dx^2} = 0.$$

The general solution is

$$y = c_1 + c_2 x.$$

Applying the first condition $y(0) = y(\pi)$, we find

$$c_1 + c_2 \cdot 0 = c_1 + c_2 \pi.$$

Thus,

$$c_2 \pi = 0,$$

which implies that $c_2 = 0$. Therefore, $y(x) = c_1$, which is a constant function. Thus, the only nontrivial solution for $\lambda = 0$ is a constant solution.

Case 2: $\lambda < 0$ For $\lambda < 0$, the characteristic equation of the differential equation is $m^2 + \lambda = 0$, with roots $\pm\sqrt{-\lambda}$. Denoting $\sqrt{-\lambda} = \alpha$, the general solution is

$$y = c_1 e^{\alpha x} + c_2 e^{-\alpha x}.$$

Applying the first condition, we obtain

$$c_1 + c_2 = c_1 e^{\alpha \pi} + c_2 e^{-\alpha \pi}.$$

For the second condition,

$$\alpha c_1 - \alpha c_2 = \alpha c_1 e^{\alpha \pi} - \alpha c_2 e^{-\alpha \pi}.$$

This system will only have nontrivial solutions if the determinant of the coefficients is zero. However, solving this system results in the conclusion that there are no nontrivial solutions when $\lambda < 0$.

Case 3: $\lambda > 0$ For $\lambda > 0$, the roots of the characteristic equation are the complex conjugates $\pm i\sqrt{\lambda}$. The general solution is

$$y = c_1 \sin(\sqrt{\lambda}x) + c_2 \cos(\sqrt{\lambda}x).$$

Applying the first condition $y(0) = y(\pi)$, we obtain

$$c_1 \sin(0) + c_2 \cos(0) = c_1 \sin(\sqrt{\lambda}\pi) + c_2 \cos(\sqrt{\lambda}\pi),$$

which simplifies to

$$c_2 = c_1 \sin(\sqrt{\lambda}\pi) + c_2 \cos(\sqrt{\lambda}\pi).$$

Next, applying the second condition $y'(0) = y'(\pi)$, we find

$$c_1\sqrt{\lambda}\cos(\sqrt{\lambda}\pi) - c_2\sqrt{\lambda}\sin(\sqrt{\lambda}\pi) = c_1\sqrt{\lambda}\cos(\sqrt{\lambda}\pi) - c_2\sqrt{\lambda}\sin(\sqrt{\lambda}\pi),$$

which gives the equation

$$\lambda = 4n^2, \text{ where } n = 0, 1, 2, 3, \ldots.$$

Conclusion: For $\lambda > 0$, the nontrivial solutions exist when $\lambda = 4n^2$, with $n = 0, 1, 2, 3, \ldots$. The corresponding solutions are

$$y = c_1 \sin(2nx) + c_2 \cos(2nx), \quad \text{where } n = 0, 1, 2, 3, \ldots.$$

5.9 Characteristic Values and Characteristic Functions

- In the given Sturm-Liouville problem, the eigenvalues are the values of λ for which there exist nontrivial solutions satisfying the supplementary conditions. As shown in the Example, the eigenvalues are determined by the condition $\lambda = n^2$, where n is a positive integer.

- The eigenfunctions corresponding to each eigenvalue $\lambda = n^2$ are given by $y_n(x) = c_n \sin(nx)$, where c_n is a nonzero constant and n is a positive integer.

Thus, the eigenvalues and eigenfunctions play a crucial role in the analysis of Sturm-Liouville problems, providing a way to decompose functions and solve differential equations subject to certain boundary conditions.

Prove that eigenvalues of a SLBVP are discrete.

Let $y_1(x, \lambda)$ and $y_2(x, \lambda)$ be two linearly independent solutions (for fixed λ) of a SLBVP consisting of a differential equation

$$\left(p(x)\frac{dy}{dx}\right)' + (q(x) + \lambda r(x))y = 0 \quad \text{with} \quad y(a) = y(b) = 0.$$

Then any solution can be expressed as a linear combination of y_1 and y_2. That is,

$$y(x, \lambda) = Ay_1(x, \lambda) + By_2(x, \lambda).$$

The constants A and B are determined by the fact that $y(x, \lambda)$ also satisfies the boundary conditions, which leads to the following system:

$$\begin{aligned} Ay_1(a, \lambda) + By_2(a, \lambda) &= 0, \\ Ay_1(b, \lambda) + By_2(b, \lambda) &= 0. \end{aligned}$$

In matrix form, this can be written as

$$\begin{pmatrix} y_1(a, \lambda) & y_2(a, \lambda) \\ y_1(b, \lambda) & y_2(b, \lambda) \end{pmatrix} \begin{pmatrix} A \\ B \end{pmatrix} = \begin{pmatrix} 0 \\ 0 \end{pmatrix}.$$

For a non-trivial solution to exist, the determinant of the matrix of coefficients must vanish. Otherwise, the only solution is $A = B = 0$, which would correspond to the trivial solution $y(x) = 0$. Thus, we have the condition:

$$\begin{vmatrix} y_1(a, \lambda) & y_2(a, \lambda) \\ y_1(b, \lambda) & y_2(b, \lambda) \end{vmatrix} = 0.$$

Since $y_1(x, \lambda)$ and $y_2(x, \lambda)$ are analytic functions of λ, the determinant itself is an analytic function of λ. According to the theory of complex-valued functions, the zeros of the determinant must be isolated. Therefore, since the zeros of the determinant correspond to solutions of the SLBVP, we conclude that the eigenvalues are discrete.

Here is a rephrased version of the provided content:

—

5.10 Orthogonality of Functions

- Two functions f and g are said to be orthogonal with respect to a weight function ω over the interval $a \le x \le b$ if and only if

$$\int_a^b f(x)g(x)\omega(x)\,dx = 0.$$

- **Example:** The functions $\sin x$ and $\sin 2x$ are orthogonal with respect to the constant weight function 1 on the interval $0 \le x \le \pi$, since

$$\int_0^\pi (\sin x)(\sin 2x)(1)\,dx = 0.$$

- Let $\{\phi_n\}_{n=1}^\infty$ represent an infinite sequence of functions defined over the interval $a \le x \le b$. This sequence is called an orthogonal system with respect to the weight function ω if each pair of distinct functions in the sequence is orthogonal with respect to ω over the interval $a \le x \le b$. In other words, the set $\{\phi_n\}$ is orthogonal with respect to ω on $a \le x \le b$ if

$$\int_a^b \phi_m(x)\phi_n(x)\omega(x)\,dx = 0 \quad \text{for}\, m \ne n.$$

- Consider the infinite set of functions $\{\phi_n\}$, where $\phi_n(x) = \sin(nx)$ for $n = 1, 2, 3, \ldots$ over the interval $0 \le x \le \pi$. This set $\{\phi_n\}$ forms an orthogonal system with respect to the weight function equal to 1 over the interval $0 \leq x \leq \pi$, as

$$\int_0^{\pi} \sin(mx)\sin(nx)\,dx = \begin{cases} 0 & \text{for } m \neq n, \\ \frac{\pi}{2} & \text{for } m = n. \end{cases}$$

5.10.1 Orthogonality of Characteristic Functions

Theorem 5.10.1. ***Sturm-Liouville Theorem:*** *Consider the Sturm-Liouville problem given by*

$$\frac{d}{dx}\left[p(x)\frac{dy}{dx}\right] + q(x)y + \lambda r(x)y = 0,$$

where p, q, and r are real functions such that p has a continuous derivative, q and r are continuous, and $p(x) > 0$ and $r(x) > 0$ for all x in the interval $a \leq x \leq b$; and λ is a constant independent of x. The boundary conditions are

$$A_1 y(a) + A_2 y'(a) = 0, \quad B_1 y(b) + B_2 y'(b) = 0,$$

where A_1, A_2, B_1, B_2 are constants, and not all of A_1, A_2 or B_1, B_2 are zero.

Theorem 5.10.2. ***Conclusion:*** *Let λ_m and λ_n be two distinct characteristic values for this problem. Let ϕ_m and ϕ_n be the characteristic functions corresponding to λ_m and λ_n, respectively. Then, the characteristic functions ϕ_m and ϕ_n are orthogonal with respect to the weight function ω on the interval $a \leq x \leq b$.*

Proof: Since ϕ_m is the characteristic function corresponding to λ_m, it satisfies the differential equation with $\lambda = \lambda_m$; and similarly, ϕ_n satisfies the differential equation with $\lambda = \lambda_n$. This gives the system of equations

$$\frac{d}{dx}\left[p(x)\frac{d\phi_m}{dx}\right] + q(x)\phi_m + \lambda_m r(x)\phi_m = 0,$$

$$\frac{d}{dx}\left[p(x)\frac{d\phi_n}{dx}\right] + q(x)\phi_n + \lambda_n r(x)\phi_n = 0.$$

Multiplying the first equation by $\phi_n(x)$ and the second by $\phi_m(x)$, then subtracting them yields

$$(\lambda_m - \lambda_n)\phi_m(x)\phi_n(x)r(x) = -\frac{d}{dx}\left[p(x)\frac{d\phi_m}{dx}\right]\phi_n + \phi_m\frac{d}{dx}\left[p(x)\frac{d\phi_n}{dx}\right].$$

Integrating both sides from a to b leads to

$$(\lambda_m - \lambda_n)\int_a^b \phi_m(x)\phi_n(x)r(x)\,dx = \int_a^b \left[p(x)\frac{d\phi_m}{dx}\right]\phi_n\,dx - \int_a^b \left[p(x)\frac{d\phi_n}{dx}\right]\phi_m\,dx.$$

Using the boundary conditions, we find that the integrals of boundary terms vanish, and thus we conclude that

$$\int_a^b r(x)\phi_m(x)\phi_n(x)\,dx = 0.$$

Therefore, ϕ_m and ϕ_n are orthogonal.

Example: Consider the Sturm-Liouville problem

$$\frac{d^2y}{dx^2} + \lambda y = 0,$$

with boundary conditions $y(0) = 0$ and $y(\pi) = 0$. The characteristic values $\lambda_n = n^2$ $(n = 1, 2, 3, \ldots)$ have corresponding characteristic functions $\phi_n(x) = c_n \sin(nx)$, where c_n is a constant. The orthogonality is given by

$$\int_0^\pi (\sin(mx))(\sin(nx))\,dx = 0 \quad \text{for} \quad m \neq n.$$

5.10.2 Orthonormal Systems

- A function f is said to be normalized with respect to a weight function ω over the interval $a \leq x \leq b$ if

$$\int_a^b (f(x))^2\,\omega(x)\,dx = 1.$$

- An orthonormal system with respect to a weight function ω over the interval

$a \leq x \leq b$ satisfies two conditions:
1. It is an orthogonal system with respect to ω on the interval $a \leq x \leq b$.
2. Every function in the system is normalized with respect to ω over the interval $a \leq x \leq b$.

Here is the rephrased version of the text to avoid plagiarism:

—

5.11 Non-Oscillatory and Oscillatory Functions

- A real-valued function $f(t)$, defined and continuous on the interval $[a, b]$, is considered non-oscillatory in $[a, b]$ if it has no more than one zero within the interval.

- A function $f(t)$ is said to be oscillatory in $[a, b]$ if it has at least two zeros within the interval.

Examples:

1. Consider the function

$$f(t) = Ae^{-t} + Be^{-t}$$

for $t \geq 0$, where A and B are constants. In this case, $f(t)$ is non-oscillatory.

2. For $f(t) = \sin t$, $t \geq 0$, it can be observed that $f(t)$ is oscillatory in the interval $[0, 4\pi]$.

5.11.1 Oscillatory and Non-Oscillatory Differential Equations

A second-order differential equation

$$\frac{d^2u}{dt^2} + p(t)\frac{du}{dt} + q(t)u = h(t), \quad t \geq 0$$

is termed "non-oscillatory" if every solution $u = u(t)$ is non-oscillatory. Otherwise, the differential equation is called oscillatory.

Example: The equation

$$u'' + u = 0$$

is oscillatory. Its general solution is

$$u(t) = A\cos t + B\sin t, \quad t \geq 0.$$

Assuming that both A and B are non-zero constants, the solution $u(t)$ exhibits oscillatory behavior and has a zero at

$$t = n\pi + \tan^{-1}\left(\frac{A}{B}\right), \quad \text{for } n = 0, 1, 2, 3, \ldots$$

Thus, this equation is oscillatory.
Example: Consider the linear equation

$$u'' - u = 0, \quad \text{for } t \geq 0.$$

Its general solution is $u(t) = Ae^t + Be^{-t}$, where A and B are constants. This solution does not exhibit oscillation and thus the equation is non-oscillatory.

Let $f(t)$ and $g(t)$ be two real-valued functions defined and continuous in the interval $[a, b]$. If $f(t)$ has more zeros in $[a, b]$ than $g(t)$ by more than one, it is said that $f(t)$ oscillates more rapidly than $g(t)$.

Example: Let $f(t) = \sin(2t)$ in $[0, 4\pi]$ and $g(t) = \sin(t)$ in $[0, 4\pi]$. The zeros of $f(t)$ are spaced half as far apart as the zeros of $g(t)$. Hence, $f(t)$ oscillates more rapidly than $g(t)$ within the interval $[0, 4\pi]$.

5.12 Riccati Equations

Consider the first-order differential equation

$$\frac{dy}{dx} = f(x, y)$$

Approximating $f(x, y)$ while x is held constant yields:

$$f(x, y) = P(x) + Q(x)y + R(x)y^2 + \dots$$

If we consider only the linear terms, the equation becomes linear. Riccati focused on approximating the equation to the second degree, leading to equations of the form:

$$\frac{dy}{dx} = P(x) + Q(x)y + R(x)y^2$$

These equations, which are nonlinear, are known as Riccati equations and do not fit into the class of classical equations.
To solve a Riccati equation, at least one particular solution is necessary. Without this, it is impossible to find a solution. Let y_1 be a particular solution.

Define a new function z as:

$$z = \frac{1}{y - y_1}$$

and the equation for z becomes

$$\frac{dz}{dx} = -(Q(x) + 2y_1 R(x))z - R(x),$$

which is now a linear equation for z.
Example:
Solve the equation

$$\frac{dy}{dx} = -2 - y + y^2$$

with the particular solution $y_1 = 2$.

Relationship Between Riccati Equation and Second-Order Linear Differential Equation:
The Riccati equation is significant in the study of differential equations because of its connection to second-order linear differential equations. Consider the

general Riccati equation:

$$\frac{dy}{dx} + Q(x)y + R(x)y^2 = P(x)$$

By making the transformation

$$y = \frac{1}{R}\frac{du}{dx} = \frac{u'}{Ru}$$

we obtain a second-order linear differential equation:

$$R\frac{d^2u}{dx^2} - (R' - QR)\frac{du}{dx} - PR^2u = 0$$

Conversely, a general homogeneous second-order linear differential equation can be transformed into a Riccati equation. Given the equation

$$A(x)\frac{d^2u}{dx^2} + B(x)\frac{du}{dx} + C(x)u = 0$$

make the transformation

$$\frac{du}{dx} = (Ry)u$$

and we obtain the Riccati equation

$$\frac{dy}{dx} + \left(\frac{R'}{R} + \frac{B}{A}\right)y + Ry^2 = \frac{-C}{AR}$$

5.13 Summary

To conclude, the Sturm-Liouville boundary value problem offers a powerful approach to analyzing various physical systems using differential equations. The Wronskian is a crucial tool for determining the linear independence of solutions, which is essential for understanding eigenvalues and eigenfunctions. Mastering these concepts provides the tools needed to address complex mathematical challenges effectively.

Chapter 6

Conclusions and Future Scope

Ordinary Differential Equations (ODEs) are a cornerstone of mathematics with extensive implications across theoretical and applied domains. This book has systematically delved into their theoretical foundations, analytical methods, and computational techniques, highlighting their vast applicability in diverse fields. The insights presented offer a comprehensive understanding of how ODEs form the backbone of many scientific explorations and real-world phenomena.

In the preceding chapters, we examined core topics such as existence and uniqueness theorems, qualitative behavior of solutions, numerical methods, and boundary value problems, including Sturm-Liouville systems. The synergy between theoretical rigor and practical implementation has been emphasized throughout. This chapter synthesizes the applications discussed and outlines future work, ensuring this exploration remains relevant and forward-looking.

6.1 Applications of Ordinary Differential Equations

ODEs have far-reaching applications across scientific disciplines. Below, we outline some key areas where ODEs play a pivotal role:

6.1.1 Physics and Engineering

- **Mechanical Systems:** ODEs govern the motion of pendulums, springs, and other mechanical oscillators. They model phenomena like damping and resonance, which are critical in engineering design.

- **Electrical Circuits:** Kirchhoff's laws lead to ODEs that describe the behavior of RLC circuits, aiding in the design of stable and efficient electrical networks.
- **Fluid Dynamics:** ODEs are foundational in describing fluid flow through Navier-Stokes equations and related simplified models for specific scenarios.

6.1.2 Biology and Medicine

- **Population Dynamics:** ODE models, such as the logistic growth equation, describe population changes, predator-prey interactions, and ecosystem stability.
- **Disease Spread:** Epidemiological models, including the SIR and SEIR frameworks, rely on ODEs to predict disease transmission and inform public health interventions.
- **Pharmacokinetics:** ODEs help determine drug concentration and its effect in the human body over time, aiding in effective dosage planning.

6.1.3 Economics and Social Sciences

- **Economic Models:** ODEs describe dynamic systems such as market fluctuations, investment growth, and resource allocation.
- **Sociological Dynamics:** Models based on ODEs analyze social phenomena, including opinion dynamics and crowd behavior.

6.1.4 Environmental Science

- **Climate Modeling:** Differential equations underpin models of temperature change, greenhouse gas effects, and weather prediction.
- **Pollution Dynamics:** ODEs are used to model pollutant dispersal in air and water, facilitating effective environmental policies.

6.1.5 Computational Science

With the advent of high-performance computing, solving complex ODEs numerically has revolutionized fields such as computational physics, bioinformatics, and artificial intelligence. Techniques such as finite difference and finite element methods enhance precision in modeling real-world systems.

6.2 Future Work and Research Directions

6.2.1 Theoretical Advances

- **Fractional Differential Equations:** Extending classical ODE frameworks to fractional-order systems opens new avenues for modeling memory-dependent and non-local phenomena.

- **Stochastic ODEs:** Incorporating randomness into differential equations enhances their ability to model systems under uncertainty, such as financial markets and climate systems.

6.2.2 Numerical Methods

- **Adaptive Algorithms:** Developing adaptive step-size algorithms for ODE solvers ensures efficiency and accuracy for stiff systems.

- **High-Dimensional Systems:** Addressing computational challenges in high-dimensional ODE systems, such as those arising in neural networks and multi-agent systems, is crucial.

6.2.3 Interdisciplinary Applications

- **Neuroscience:** Modeling brain activity and neural networks using ODEs offers insights into cognition and neurological disorders.

- **Sustainability:** ODEs can model resource consumption and renewable energy dynamics, aiding in sustainable development planning.

6.2.4 Integration with Machine Learning

The integration of ODEs with machine learning frameworks has emerged as a transformative direction. Neural ODEs, which combine the structure of differential equations with data-driven learning, have shown promise in predictive analytics and control systems.

The study of Ordinary Differential Equations remains a vibrant and expanding field. Its intersection with cutting-edge disciplines such as machine learning, quantum mechanics, and synthetic biology underscores its enduring relevance. By addressing both foundational aspects and emerging challenges, this book aims to inspire continued exploration and innovation in the domain of ODEs.

References

[1] P. Hartman, *Ordinary differential equations.* SIAM, 2002.

[2] E. L. Ince, *Ordinary differential equations.* Courier Corporation, 1956.

[3] V. I. Arnold, *Ordinary differential equations.* Springer Science & Business Media, 1992.

[4] R. K. Miller and A. N. Michel, *Ordinary differential equations.* Academic press, 2014.

[5] K. Bansal, T. Mathur, N. S. S. Singh, and S. Agarwal, "Analysis of illegal drug transmission model using fractional delay differential equations," *AIMS Mathematics*, vol. 7, no. 10, pp. 18173–18193, 2022.

[6] K. Bansal, S. Arora, K. S. Pritam, T. Mathur, and S. Agarwal, "Dynamics of crime transmission using fractional-order differential equations," *Fractals*, vol. 30, p. 2250012, 2022.

[7] K. Bansal, T. Mathur, and S. Agarwal, "Fractional-order crime propagation model with non-linear transmission rate," *Chaos, Solitons & Fractals*, vol. 169, p. 113321, 2023.

[8] K. Bansal, T. Mathur, T. Mathur, S. Agarwal, and R. D. Sharma, "Impact of social media on academics: a fractional order mathematical model," *International Journal of Modelling and Simulation*, pp. 1–15, 2023.

[9] K. Bansal, T. Mathur, and S. Agarwal, "The ladm approach to analyze the fractional order model for smoking habits including memory," in *AIP Conference Proceedings*, vol. 2819, AIP Publishing, 2023.

[10] K. Bansal and T. Mathur, "Impact of skills development on youth unemployment: A fractional-order mathematical model," *Mathematical Methods in the Applied Sciences*, 2024.

[11] G. Pathan and P. Bhathawala, "Unemployment-discussion with a mathematical model," *International Journal of Business Management and Economic Research*, vol. 3, pp. 19–27, 2016.

[12] S. A. Veronica and A. U. Samuel, "Social media addiction among adolescents with special reference to Facebook addiction," *IOSR Journal of Humanities and Social Science (IOSR-JHSS)*, vol. 4, pp. 72–76, 2015.

[13] A. Carvalho and C. M. Pinto, "A delay fractional order model for the co-infection of malaria and HIV/AIDS," *International Journal of Dynamics and Control*, vol. 5, no. 1, pp. 168–186, 2017.

[14] L. A. Gil-Alana, Z. A. Ozdemir, and A. Tansel, "Long memory in Turkish unemployment rates," *Emerging Markets Finance and Trade*, vol. 55, no. 1, pp. 201–217, 2019.

[15] A. Chalfin and J. McCrary, "Criminal deterrence: A review of the literature," *Journal of Economic Literature*, vol. 55, no. 1, pp. 5–48, 2017.

[16] R. M. Al-Maalwi, H. Ashi, and S. Al-sheikh, "Unemployment model," *Applied Mathematical Sciences*, vol. 12, no. 21, pp. 989–1006, 2018.

[17] R. K. Sah, "Social osmosis and patterns of crime," *Journal of Political Economy*, vol. 99, no. 6, pp. 1272–1295, 1991.

[18] S. Abbas, J. P. Tripathi, and A. Neha, "Dynamical analysis of a model of social behavior: Criminal vs non-criminal population," *Chaos, Solitons & Fractals*, vol. 98, pp. 121–129, 2017.

[19] H. T. Alemneh and N. Y. Alemu, "Mathematical modeling with optimal control analysis of social media addiction," *Infectious Disease Modelling*, vol. 6, pp. 405–419, 2021.

[20] B. Berenji, T. Chou, and M. R. D'Orsogna, "Recidivism and rehabilitation of criminal offenders: A carrot and stick evolutionary game," *Plos One*, vol. 9, no. 1, p. e85531, 2014.

[21] A. Blumstein and R. Larson, "Models of a total criminal justice system," *Operations Research*, vol. 17, no. 2, pp. 199–232, 1969.

[22] S. Tomsen, *Violence, prejudice and sexuality*. Routledge, 2013.

[23] R. Tarling, "Unemployment and crime," *Home Office Research Bulletin*, vol. 14, pp. 28–33, 1982.

[24] T. Kamal, M. Ishtiaq, K. Nawab, and M. Idrees, "An investigation into the negative impacts of social media on academic performance of youth," *New Media and Mass Communication*, vol. 34, pp. 50–56, 2015.

[25] M. Habes, M. Alghizzawi, R. Khalaf, S. A. Salloum, and M. A. Ghani, "The relationship between social media and academic performance: Facebook perspective," *International Journal of Information Technology and Language Studies*, vol. 2, no. 1, pp. 12–18, 2018.

[26] N. T. Bailey, *The mathematical theory of infectious diseases and its applications*. Charles Griffin & Company Ltd, 5a Crendon Street, High Wycombe, Bucks HP13 6LE, 1975.

[27] D. Baleanu, H. Mohammadi, and S. Rezapour, "A mathematical theoretical study of a particular system of caputo–fabrizio fractional differential equations for the rubella disease model," *Advances in Difference Equations*, vol. 2020, no. 1, pp. 1–19, 2020.

[28] N. Crokidakis, "Modeling the impact of civilian firearm ownership in the evolution of violent crimes," *Applied Mathematics and Computation*, vol. 429, p. 127256, 2022.

[29] W. Ding, R. Hendon, B. Cathey, E. Lancaster, and R. Germick, "Discrete time optimal control applied to pest control problems," *Involve, a Journal of Mathematics*, vol. 7, no. 4, pp. 479–489, 2014.

[30] K. Diethelm, "Efficient solution of multi-term fractional differential equations using p (ec) m e methods," *Computing*, vol. 71, no. 4, pp. 305–319, 2003.

[31] S. E. Eikenberry and A. B. Gumel, "Mathematical modeling of climate change and malaria transmission dynamics: A historical review," *Journal of Mathematical Biology*, vol. 77, no. 4, pp. 857–933, 2018.

[32] K. Gehring, T. Kauffeldt, and K. C. Vadlamannati, "Crime, incentives and political effort: A model and empirical application for India," *Available at SSRN 2892255*, 2016.

[33] W. Walter, *Ordinary differential equations*, vol. 182. Springer Science & Business Media, 2013.

[34] E. A. Coddington, *An introduction to ordinary differential equations*. Courier Corporation, 2012.

[35] G. M. Murphy, *Ordinary differential equations and their solutions*. Courier Corporation, 2011.

[36] R. P. Agarwal, D. O'Regan, *et al.*, *An introduction to ordinary differential equations*. Springer, 2008.

[37] J. Kurzweil, *Ordinary differential equations: introduction to the theory of ordinary differential equations in the real domain*. Elsevier, 2014.

[38] R. Grimshaw, *Nonlinear ordinary differential equations*. Routledge, 2017.

[39] J. P. LaSalle, "Stability theory for ordinary differential equations," *Journal of Differential equations*, vol. 4, no. 1, pp. 57–65, 1968.

www.ingramcontent.com/pod-product-compliance
Lightning Source LLC
LaVergne TN
LVHW070229170826
845679LV00035B/1876

9798896997016